Kindle Fire™ HD

FOR

DUMMIES®

Kindle Fire™ HD

FOR

DUMMIES®

by Nancy C. Muir

WILEY

John Wiley & Sons, Inc.

Kindle Fire™ HD For Dummies®

Published by
John Wiley & Sons, Inc.
111 River Street
Hoboken, NJ 07030-5774
www.wiley.com

WILEY

About the Author

Nancy Muir is the author of over 100 technology books on topics ranging from tablet computers and popular computer applications to nanotechnology. Her website TechSmart Senior (`www.techsmartsenior.com`) provides information for those reading her bestselling *Computers For Seniors For Dummies* and *Laptops For Seniors For Dummies* books (both published by Wiley) and others discovering technology later in their lives. She contributes a column on computers and the Internet at `www.retirenet.com`. Prior to her writing career, Nancy was a manager in both the publishing and computer software industries.

Dedication

To Blair Pottenger, my partner in crime for the last seven years or so, for his unending professionalism and support.

Author's Acknowledgments

I could not have written this book without the help and support of many people. I must thank Katie Mohr, Senior Acquisitions Editor extraordinaire, who jumped through many hoops to make this book happen and had faith in my ability to write this book. Blair Pottenger performed heroic editorial feats by juggling several of my books on a very fast-paced schedule. The copy editor, Laura Miller, worked on a very fast schedule to make this the best book it could be.

Publisher's Acknowledgments

We're proud of this book; please send us your comments at http://dummies.custhelp.com. For other comments, please contact our Customer Care Department within the U.S. at 877-762-2974, outside the U.S. at 317-572-3993, or fax 317-572-4002.

Some of the people who helped bring this book to market include the following:

Acquisitions and Editorial

Project Editor: Blair J. Pottenger

Senior Acquisitions Editor: Katie Mohr

Copy Editor: Laura K. Miller

Editorial Manager: Kevin Kirschner

Editorial Assistant: Leslie Saxman

Sr. Editorial Assistant: Cherie Case

Composition Services

Project Coordinator: Patrick Redmond

Layout and Graphics: Jennifer Creasey, Joyce Haughey, Laura Westhuis

Proofreaders: Debbye Butler, Susan Moritz

Indexer: Ty Koontz

Publishing and Editorial for Technology Dummies

Richard Swadley, Vice President and Executive Group Publisher

Andy Cummings, Vice President and Publisher

Mary Bednarek, Executive Acquisitions Director

Mary C. Corder, Editorial Director

Publishing for Consumer Dummies

Kathleen Nebenhaus, Vice President and Executive Publisher

Composition Services

Debbie Stailey, Director of Composition Services

Contents at a Glance

Table of Contents

Part III: Having Fun and Getting Productive 125

Chapter 6: E-Reader Extraordinaire 127

Chapter 7: Playing Music 151

Chapter 8: Playing Video....................................167

Introduction

Kindle Fire HD is a very affordable way to get at all kinds of media, from music and videos to books and colorful magazines. It's also a device that allows you to browse the Internet, connect to your Facebook account, make video calls via Skype, check your e-mail, and read documents. Its portability makes it incredibly useful for people on the go in today's fast-paced world.

In this book, I introduce you to all the cool features of Kindle Fire HD, providing tips and advice for getting the most out of this ingenious little tablet. I help you find your way around its attractive and easy-to-use interface, provide advice about getting the most out of the Amazon Cloud Drive for storing content, and even recommend some neat apps that make your device more functional and fun.

Why Buy This Book?

"If Kindle Fire HD is so easy to use, why do I need a book?" you may be asking yourself. When I first sat down with Kindle Fire HD, it took about three or four days of poking around to find settings, features, and ways to buy and locate my content and apps. When was the last time you had four days to spare? I've spent the time so that you can quickly and easily get the hang of all the Kindle Fire HD features and discover a few tricks I bet your friends won't uncover for quite a while.

This book covers many of the features in the original Kindle Fire, released in 2011, as well as the features that are new with the Kindle Fire HD. In September 2012, Amazon also released a new, upgraded (though non-HD) version of the first-generation Kindle Fire that costs $159 and has only 8GB of storage, along with the somewhat clunkier hardware design of the original Kindle Fire. Though this book is focused on Kindle Fire HD, whichever Kindle Fire model you own, you should find lots of advice and answers in this book.

Foolish Assumptions

You may have opted for a tablet to watch movies and read books on the run. You might think it's a good way to browse business documents and check e-mail on your next plane trip. You might have one or more computers and be very computer savvy, or you might hate computers and figure that Kindle Fire HD gives you all the computing power you need to browse the Internet and read e-books.

Kindle Fire HD users come in all types. I won't assume in this book that you're a computer whiz, but I will assume that you have a passing understanding of how to copy a file and plug in a USB cable. I'm guessing you've browsed the Internet at least a few times and heard of Wi-Fi, which is what you use to go online with a Kindle Fire HD (unless you purchase the 8.9-inch LTE version). Other than that, you don't need a lot of technical background to get the most out of this book.

How This Book Is Organized

For Dummies books don't require a linear read, meaning that you could jump in anywhere and find out what you need to know about a particular feature. However, if you're opening the box and starting from square one with your Kindle Fire HD, consider working through the first couple of chapters first. Here's the breakdown for how this book is organized.

Part I: Making the Kindle Fire HD Yours

This part provides information about what's new in Kindle Fire HD and how to set up your Kindle Fire HD out of the box. You begin to understand how to navigate your way around the device and get things done using its simple interface. You also discover how to make some of the most useful Kindle Fire HD settings, such as adjusting volume and screen brightness and managing Parental Controls.

Part II: Taking the Leap Online

Chapters 4 and 5 help you buy apps and media content, such as music, videos, and magazines. You also explore how to go online and set up your e-mail account and Wi-Fi connection, and work with the Silk browser.

Part III: Having Fun and Getting Productive

In this part, you can begin to explore the wealth of multimedia and written content Kindle Fire HD makes available to you. You get to know the Kindle e-reader and how to subscribe to and read periodicals; you also find out how all this content is coordinated among your devices using Amazon's Whispersync technology. Chapters 7 and 8 are where you read about playing music and videos on your Kindle Fire HD. Chapter 9 gets you connected to others as you manage contacts, and make calls over the Internet using Kindle Fire HD and the Skype app, while Chapter 10 talks about getting productive by working with documents.

Part IV: The Part of Tens

This part includes two chapters that recommend apps you can get to add basic functionality to the Kindle Fire HD, such as a calculator and notes, and ten games to turn your Kindle Fire HD into a great gaming machine.

Icons Used in This Book

Icons are little pictures in the margin of this book that alert you to special types of advice or information, including

✓ These short words of advice draw your attention to faster, easier, or alternative ways of getting things done with Kindle Fire HD. Tips might also point out where a feature works slightly different from the first generation Kindle Fire or another Kindle Fire HD model.

✓ When you see this icon, you'll know that I'm emphasizing important information for you to keep in mind as you use a feature.

✓ There aren't too many ways you can get in trouble with the Kindle Fire HD, but in those few situations where some action might be irreversible, I include warnings so you can avoid any pitfalls.

Get Going!

Time to get that Kindle Fire HD out of its box, set it up, and get going with all the fun, entertaining things it makes available to you. Have fun!

Part I
Making the Kindle Fire HD Yours

The 5th Wave — By Rich Tennant

"Other than this little glitch with the landscape view, I really love my Kindle Fire HD."

In this part . . .

This part provides information about what's new in Kindle Fire HD and how to set up your Kindle Fire HD out of the box. You begin to understand how to navigate your way around the device and get things done using its simple interface. You also discover how to make some of the most useful Kindle Fire HD settings, such as adjusting volume and screen brightness and managing Parental Controls.

1

Overview of the Kindle Fire HD

*A*mazon, the giant online retailer, just happens to have access to more content (music, movies, audio books, and so on) than just about anybody on the planet. So, when an Amazon tablet was rumored to be in the works, and as Amazon stacked up media partnerships with the likes of Fox and PBS, the mystery tablet was seen as the first real challenge to Apple's iPad.

Now, a year after the release of the first Kindle Fire, the Kindle Fire HD is available, and it turns out to offer several very nice improvements at the right price and feature mix for many people, while offering the key to that treasure chest of content Amazon has been wise enough to amass.

In this chapter, you get an overview of the Kindle Fire HD: how it compares to competing devices and its key features. Subsequent chapters delve into how to use all those features.

A Quick Rundown of Kindle Fire HD Hardware Features

Let's start at the beginning. A *tablet* is a handheld computer with a touchscreen and an onscreen keyboard for providing input, and apps that allow you to play games, read e-books, check e-mail, browse the web, watch movies and buy music, and more.

In the world of tablets, the first device to hit big was iPad, and then subsequent tablets, such as Samsung Galaxy and HP TouchPad, appeared. No tablet since iPad seemed to have gained a foothold in the market until Kindle Fire showed up.

Kindle Fire HD, the second generation of Kindle Fire, is lighter and smaller than iPad, at $7.6 \times 5.4 \times 0.4$ inches (see Figure 1-1) and weighing only 13.9 ounces, versus iPad's 9.7-inch display and 1.3-pound frame. For some, that smaller, lighter form factor makes the Kindle Fire HD easier to hold with one hand than the iPad. In addition, the rubberized back helps you keep a tight grip on the device, in most circumstances.

Kindle Fire HD has a projected battery life of 11 hours. The screen resolution on the Kindle Fire HD's bright color screen is just about on a par with the best tablets out there, and it brings the addition of gorilla glass, which means the screen is tough and probably doesn't require an additional screen protector.

Photo courtesy of Amazon.com

Figure 1-1: The neat size and weight of Kindle Fire HD make it easy to hold.

In its first generation model, Kindle Fire had no camera or microphone, which meant you couldn't use it to take pictures or make phone calls. With the arrival of Kindle Fire HD, you have a camera and microphone that allow you to make video calls with the built-in Skype app. However, there still isn't what you'd think of a traditional camera, one that allows you to take still photos or videos, as you can with some other popular tablets.

Finally, though a Micro USB cable (one end is a standard USB connector that fits in your computer and the other end is a micro USB connector that fits into Kindle Fire HD) is included with the Kindle Fire HD, there's no power adapter for plugging it into an outlet and charging it. You can buy an adapter from Amazon for about $10 when you buy your device or $20 if you buy it separately. Alternately, you can root around in your kitchen drawer to see if you have ever owned a smartphone that came with such an adapter. The adapter simply plugs into the USB end of the Micro USB cable.

Table 1-1 provides an at-a-glance view of Kindle Fire HD features.

Table 1-1	Kindle Fire HD Specifications
Feature	*Kindle Fire HD Specs*
Display size	7 inches or 8.9 inches
Processor	Dual Core Omap 4470 processor
Screen resolution	1900 × 1200
Internal storage	16GB or 32GB
Battery life	11 hours
Price	7-inch model is $199 for 16GB and $249 for 32GB; 8.9-inch model is $299 for 16GB and $369 for 32GB
Content	Amazon Appstore
Connectivity	Wi-Fi
Ports	Micro USB to connect to your computer, HDMI port for high definition video output
Browser	Silk
Camera	For video calls only
Sound	Dual stereo speakers, Dolby Digital Plus sound
Volume control	Physical volume rocker switch
Antenna	Dual band, dual antenna for Wi-Fi

Key Features of Kindle Fire HD

Kindle Fire HD is a tablet device with all the things most people want from a tablet packed into an easy-to-hold package: e-mail, web browsing, players for video and music content, built-in calendar and contacts apps, an e-reader, a great online content store, access to tens of thousands of Android apps, and so on. In the following sections, you get to explore all these useful features.

Storage on Earth and in the cloud

Kindle Fire HD offers 16GB and 32GB of storage in its 7-inch model. Either storage amount will probably work just fine for you because when you own a Kindle Fire HD, you get free, unlimited Amazon Cloud Drive storage for all digital content purchased from Amazon (but not content that you copy onto Kindle Fire HD from your computer by connecting a Micro USB cable). This means that books, movies, music, and apps are held online for you to stream or download at any time, instead of being stored on your Kindle Fire HD.

This Amazon Cloud Drive storage means that you don't use up your Kindle Fire HD memory. As long as you have a Wi-Fi connection, you can stream content from Amazon Cloud at any time. If you'll be away from a connection, download an item (such as an episode of your favorite TV show) and watch it, and then remove it from your device the next time you're within range of a Wi-Fi network. The content is still available in the Cloud: You can download that content again or stream it anytime you like.

If you want to go whole hog into Kindle Fire HD Land, you can opt for the highest memory device, the 64GB 8.9-inch Kindle Fire HD 4G LTE Wireless version of the device. Just be aware that this version comes with the cost of an AT&T data plan.

App appeal

In several ways, Kindle Fire HD is easy to use, with a simple Android-based touchscreen interface. It's a great device for consuming media — and what a lot of media Amazon makes available! Kindle Fire HD also offers a brand new version of its Silk browser, an e-mail client, calendar and contact apps, and an available Skype app, as well as the Kindle e-reader (see Figure 1-2).

Just because a particular type of app doesn't come preinstalled on Kindle Fire HD doesn't mean you can't get one, often for free. At this point, the selection of apps available for Android devices isn't nearly as robust as those available for Apple devices, but that will change over time. See Chapter 11 for a list of ten apps that can flesh out your Kindle Fire HD with popular features such as a budget tracker, weather reporter, and calculator, and check out Chapter 12 for ten or so great game apps.

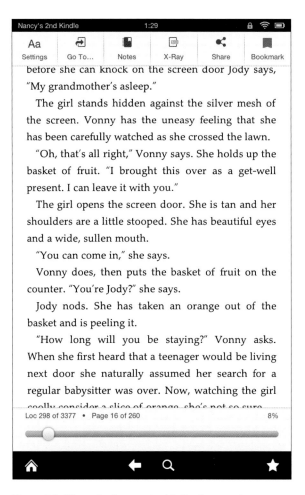

Figure 1-2: Where it all started, with Kindle e-reader functionality.

Check out the price

Amazon brought the Kindle Fire to market as a lower-priced device, losing money on the hardware and making it up with content purchases. Some consider it just a device for buying Amazon content, and it certainly lacks some features of more sophisticated devices such as iPad. However, the lower pricing scheme has clearly been a hit with many people.

Here's the rundown of current Kindle Fire devices and their pricing:

- **Kindle Fire:** $159
- **Kindle Fire HD 7-inch display:** 16GB, $199; 32GB, $249
- **Kindle Fire HD 8.9-inch display:** 16GB, $299; 32GB, $369
- **Kindle Fire HD 8.9-inch display with 4G LTE Wireless:** 32GB, $499; 64GB, $599

Just keep in mind that at the top end, you'll pay $829 for a 9.7-inch, 64GB, 3G iPad and $599 for a 64GB Kindle Fire HD 8.9-inch 4G LTE Wireless. Amazon is positioning its device as a more cost-effective tablet, but do be aware that the lower cost on the Kindle Fire HD is subsidized to some extent by some rather blatant advertising. You can pay $15 to have the advertising removed from your Kindle Fire HD experience. See Chapter 3 for more about how to do this.

Pre-installed functionality

Here's a rundown of the functionality you get out of the box from pre-installed apps:

- E-reader to read both books and periodicals
- Music player
- Video player
- Audiobook player
- Contacts app
- Calendar app
- Cube Calculator app
- Docs document reader for Word, PDF, RTF, and HTML format files
- Silk web browser
- Photos (see Figure 1-3) in which you can view and make a very few edits (rotate and crop) to photos
- Personal Videos app for transferring personal videos to Kindle Fire HD
- The IMDb database of movie trivia and facts
- E-mail client (use this to set up Kindle Fire HD to access your existing e-mail accounts)
- Integration for Facebook and Twitter
- OfficeSuite for simple word processing and spreadsheet functionality

Figure 1-3: Use the Photos app to view photos you copy from your computer to Kindle Fire HD.

Check out the apps stored on the cloud (meaning that these apps are stored at Amazon, rather than being pre-installed on your device) by tapping Apps on the Home screen and then tapping the Cloud tab. Here, you may find a number of free apps, such as a Wi-Fi analyzer (to check your Wi-Fi connection), free games, and more.

Kindle Fire HD gives you the ability to

- ⦿ Shop at Amazon for music, video, apps, books, and periodicals, and view or play that content.

- ⦿ Store Amazon-purchased content in the Amazon Cloud Drive and play music and video selections from the Cloud, instead of downloading them to your device. Amazon content doesn't count towards your Amazon Cloud Drive storage limit (20GB), but other content backed up there does. Note that you can go to www.amazon.com/clouddrive and purchase anywhere from 50GB for $25 up to 1000GB of storage for $500.

- ⦿ Send documents to yourself at a Kindle e-mail address that's assigned when you register your device (see Chapter 2 for more about setting up your Kindle Fire HD, and Chapter 10 for more about using your Kindle Fire e-mail address to send documents to your Kindle Fire HD).

- ⦿ *Sideload* (transfer) content from your computer to your Kindle Fire HD by using a Micro USB cable that comes with Kindle Fire HD. Using this cable (see Figure 1-4), you can copy photos, music, videos, and documents (Word or PDF) from any computer onto your Kindle Fire HD.

    Although the Micro USB cable shown in Figure 1-4 is included with the Kindle Fire HD, the power adapter isn't; you have to purchase the power adapter separately.

- ⦿ Make video calls using the free Skype for Kindle Fire HD app.

Figure 1-4: The Kindle Fire HD's Micro USB cable and a power adapter (sold separately).

The magic of Whispersync

If you've ever owned a Kindle e-reader, you know that downloading Amazon content to it has always been seamless. All you need for this process is access to a Wi-Fi network. Then, you simply order a book, music, or a video, and within moments, it appears on your Kindle device.

Kindle Fire HD enjoys the same kind of easy download capability via Amazon's Whispersync technology for books, audiobooks, music, video, and periodicals.

Whispersync also helps sync items such as bookmarks you've placed in e-books or the last place you watched in a video across various devices. For example, say you have the Kindle e-reader app on your Kindle Fire HD, PC, and smartphone. Wherever you left off reading, whatever notes you entered, and whatever pages you've bookmarked will be synced among all the devices without you having to lift a finger.

A great addition with Kindle Fire HD is something called Immersion Reading. This feature means that you play an audiobook and have the current word that's being spoken highlighted in the text. This feature supposedly aids in reader retention, so it might be a nice match for those late-night study sessions with textbooks.

Content, content, content!

Kindle Fire HD is meant to be a device you use to consume media, meaning that you can play/read all kinds of music, movies, TV shows, podcasts, e-books, audiobooks, magazines, and newspapers. Amazon has built up a huge amount of content, from print (see Figure 1-5) to audio books (over 22 million) to movies, TV shows, songs, books, magazines, audiobooks, apps, and games. Count on these numbers to have risen by the time you read this: Amazon continues to rack up deals with media groups such as Fox Broadcasting and PBS to make even more content available on a regular basis.

Tap on a library — such as Books, Music, or Videos — on the Kindle Fire HD Home screen, and you can find various kinds of content in the Amazon store by tapping the Store button. Tap Newsstand to shop for periodicals (see Figure 1-6) and Music to shop for songs and albums, tap Video and you go directly to the Amazon VideoStore, and tap Apps to shop the Amazon Appstore. All the content you purchase is backed up on the Amazon Cloud Drive.

When you own a Kindle you can take advantage of the Kindle Owner's Lending Library, where you can choose from over 190,000 books to borrow at no charge for as long as you like. If you have an Amazon Prime membership, you can also get one free book a month for your permanent library.

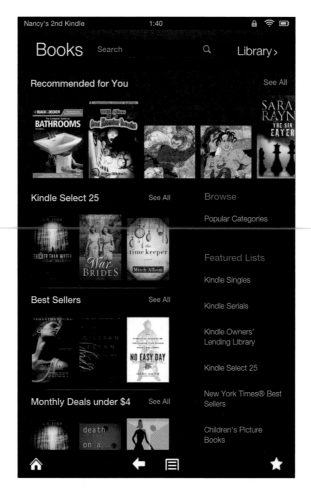

Figure 1-5: The Kindle Store offers more than 1 million books for the Kindle e-reader app.

If you're concerned about kids who access content over your Kindle Fire HD, check out the limitations you can place using Parental Controls (see in Chapter 3).

See Chapter 4 for more about buying content and apps for your Kindle Fire HD.

You can also transfer documents from your computer or send them via e-mail and read them on Kindle Fire HD or share them via the Amazon Cloud Drive. Note, however, that docs aren't backed up in Amazon Cloud Drive as music, books, and videos are.

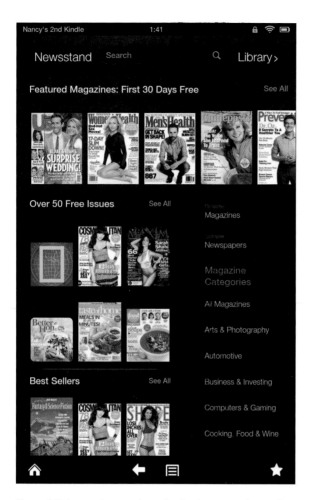

Figure 1-6: Amazon's magazine selection is constantly growing.

Browsing with Amazon Silk

Silk is Kindle Fire HD's browser (see Figure 1-7). Silk is simple to use, but the real benefits of Amazon Silk are all about browsing performance.

Amazon Silk is touted as a "Cloud-accelerated split browser." In plain English, this means that the browser can use the power of Amazon's servers to load the pages of a website quickly. Because parts of the process of loading web pages are handled not on your Kindle Fire HD, but on servers in the Cloud, your pages are supposed to display faster.

Figure 1-7: Amazon Silk offers simple-to-use browsing tools.

In addition, you get what's called a *persistent connection,* which means that your tablet is always connected to the Amazon Internet backbone (the routes that data travels to move among networks online) whenever it has access to a Wi-Fi connection.

The Kindle Fire HD 7-inch and 8.9-inch models can connect only via Wi-Fi; the 8.9-inch Kindle Fire HD 4G LTE Wireless model is the only one that has Wi-Fi access and 4G LTE access, so it can connect to a cellular network just as your mobile phone does.

But is it private?

There were some early misgivings about privacy and the Silk browser when the original Kindle Fire was released in 2011. Folks were concerned about the fact that Amazon collects information about browsing habits in order to predict what page most folks were likely to browse to next.

These fears were allayed when Amazon assured the press and others that they don't collect personally identifiable information (meaning they note that a user clicked a particular link but don't keep a record of which user did so), nor do they use this information for anything other than to produce a better browsing experience.

Another touted ability of Silk is the way it filters content to deliver it faster. Say you open a news site, such as MSN or CNN. Obviously, millions of others are accessing these pages on the same day. If most of those folks choose to open the Entertainment page after reading the home page of the site, Silk essentially predicts what page you might open next and pre-loads it. If you choose to go to that page, too, it appears instantly.

A world of color on the durable display

The display on Kindle Fire HD offers a 1280-x-800 HD display (see Figure 1-8). The high-resolution screen makes for very crisp colors when you're watching that hit movie or reading a colorful magazine. *In-plane switching* is a technology that gives you a wide viewing angle on the Kindle Fire HD screen. The result is that, if you want to share your movie with a friend sitting next to you on the couch, she'll have no problem seeing what's on the screen from that side angle.

In addition, the gorilla-glass screen is coated with layers that make it extra strong, so it should withstand most of the bumps and scratches you throw at it.

Of course, you should avoid dropping your Kindle Fire HD, exposing it to extreme temperatures, or spilling liquids on it. The User Guide also advises that, if you do spill liquids, you shouldn't heat the device in your microwave to dry it off. (Perhaps a case of tablet maintenance advice for real dummies?)

Note that Kindle Fire HD, although it has a screen that renders images crisply, is not, technically, a high-definition device. Although you can purchase and play HD versions of movies and TV shows — and Kindle Fire HD offers enough pixels to play your video in high definition — most of those pixels are used to display your image in letterbox format (a black border around an image). See Chapter 8 for more about playing video content.

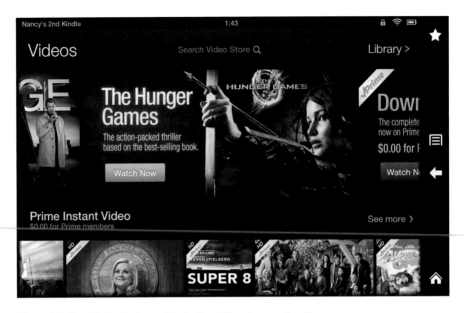

Figure 1-8: The bright display on Kindle Fire HD makes media shine.

Understanding the value of Amazon Prime

Kindle Fire HD comes with one free month of Amazon Prime. I've been an Amazon Prime member for years, so I can tell you firsthand that this service is one of the best deals out there. During your free month, Prime will allow you to get a lot of perks, such as free two-day shipping on thousands of items sold through Amazon, a free e-book, and free instant videos.

If you decide to pick up the service after your free month, it will cost you $79 a year. So, what do you get for your money?

Prime includes free two-day shipping on millions of items and overnight shipping for only $3.99. Not every item offered on Amazon is eligible for Prime, but enough are that it's a wonderful savings in time and money over the course of a year. You can probably pay for the membership with the free shipping on the first two or three orders you place. And getting your Prime stuff in only two days every time is sweet.

In addition, Prime membership gives you access to Prime Instant Videos (see Figure 1-9), which includes thousands of movies and TV shows that can be streamed to your Kindle Fire HD absolutely free. We're not talking obscure 1970s sleepers here: Recent additions to Prime Instant Videos include TV shows such as *Downton Abbey* and *Parks and Recreations,* and award winning movies such as *Rango* and *True Grit.*

Figure 1-9: The Prime Instant Videos service adds new videos all the time; check it out!

If you have already paid for a yearly subscription to Amazon Prime, you don't get an extra month for free, sad to say. And if you don't have a Prime account, your 30 days of a free account starts from the time you activate your Kindle Fire HD, not the first time you make a Prime purchase or stream a Prime Instant Video. So, my suggestion is to start using it right away to take full advantage and decide whether the paid membership is for you.

2

Kindle Fire HD Quickstart

*T*he basics of using Kindle Fire HD are . . . well, pretty basic. You start by turning it on and following a set of extremely short and simple instructions to set it up and register it, and then you can begin to get acquainted with its features.

In this chapter, I help you to get familiar with what comes in the box, explore the interface (what you see on the screen), and start to use your fingers to interact with the touchscreen. Finally, to round out your introduction to Kindle Fire HD basics, you begin to get a sense of how things are organized on Kindle Fire HD's Home screen.

Get Going with Kindle Fire HD

There's always a logical place to start building a fire. In this case, forget the logs and matches, and get started by examining what comes in the Kindle Fire HD box and learn how to turn your nifty new device on and off. The first time you turn on Kindle Fire HD, you register it and link it to your Amazon account so you can shop till you drop.

Also, although your device probably comes with a decent battery charge, at some point, you'll inevitably have to charge the battery, so I cover that in the section "Charging the battery," later in this chapter, as well.

Opening the box

When your Kindle Fire HD arrives, it will come in a dark gray box (see Figure 2-1). The Kindle Fire HD itself rests on top of a piece of hard plastic, and a small black card with some Kindle Fire HD basics printed on both sides is slotted into the lid of the box. Finally, beneath the piece of plastic rests a Micro USB cable in a paper sleeve that you use to connect the device to a computer. That's it.

Remove the protective plastic from the device, and you're ready to get going.

Figure 2-1: The Kindle Fire HD packaging.

Turning your Kindle Fire HD on and off

After you get the tablet out of its packaging, it's time to turn it on. The Kindle Fire HD sports a Power button on the top edge of the device when you hold it in portrait orientation (see Figure 2-2). Next to the Power button is the volume rocker, as well as a headphone jack. On the right side of the device is a Micro USB port, where you can insert the Micro USB cable to connect the Kindle Fire HD to your computer and an HDMI port for sending video out to a TV; the camera is located on the left side of the device.

Camera

Headphone jack   Volume rocker   Power button

Micro USB port

HDMI port

Photo courtesy of Amazon.com

Figure 2-2: The Power button sits on the top of your Kindle Fire HD.

To turn the device on, press the Power button (it can be a bit tricky to find, so you may have to turn the device so that you can see the switches on the top; the Power button is roughly in the middle). If you're starting up for the first time, you're taken through a series of setup screens (see "Setting Up Your Kindle Fire HD," later in this chapter for more about this). After you go through the setup process and register your Kindle Fire HD, you'll see the Home screen shown in Figure 2-3 on startup. The Status bar gives you information about items such as your device's battery charge, as well as access to a Quick Settings menu for universal Kindle Fire HD settings; the Favorites button (the star in the bottom-right corner of the screen) provides access to Favorite apps (the Silk browser, Mail, Help, and the IMDb database are here by default, but you can add other apps or items such as books at any time). You can find more about the elements on the Home screen in the section "Getting to Know the Interface," later in this chapter.

If you want to lock your Kindle Fire HD, which is akin to putting a laptop computer to sleep, press the Power button again. To shut down your Kindle, press and hold the Power button until a message appears offering you the options to Shut Down or Cancel, as shown in Figure 2-4.

If your Kindle Fire HD becomes non-responsive, you can press and hold the Power button for 20 seconds, and it should come to life again.

If you own an original Kindle Fire, you'll find the Power button, Micro USB port, and headset jack along the bottom of the device. With this set up, remember that you can accidentally press the Power button when you place Kindle Fire on a table or other surface, which turns it off.

Getting to know the touchscreen

Before you work through the setup screens for your Kindle Fire HD, it will help if you to get to know the basics of navigating the touchscreen — especially if you've never used a touchscreen before:

- ✔ Swipe down from the status bar at the top of the Home screen to display Quick Settings; swipe up to hide the Quick Settings.

- ✔ Tap an item to select it or double-tap an item (such as an app) to open it.

- ✔ If your Kindle Fire HD goes to a lock screen after a period of inactivity, swipe the Unlock button (see Figure 2-5) from right to left to go to the Home screen. You can also swipe the Special Offers button from left to right to see details about the latest Amazon offer displayed there. When you reach the ad screen, tap the Home button (the one shaped like a little house) to go to the Home screen.

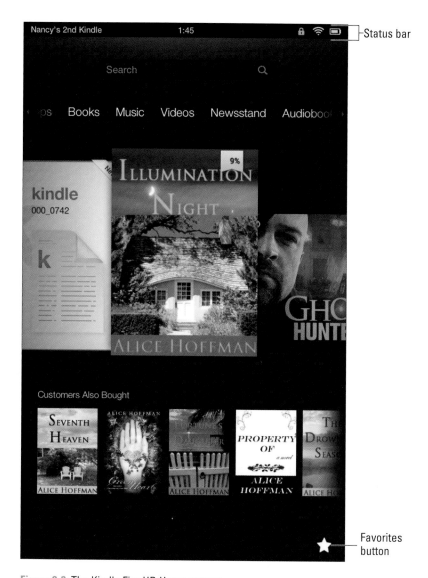

Figure 2-3: The Kindle Fire HD Home screen.

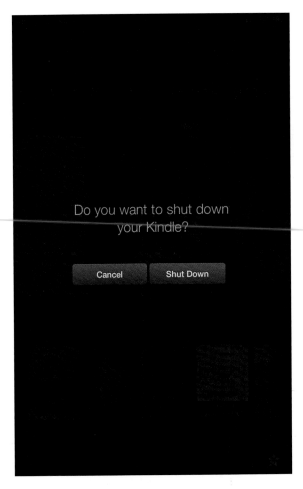

Figure 2-4: You can proceed to shut down your device, or cancel and return to the Home screen.

✔ Double-tap the screen to enlarge text and double-tap again to return the text to its original size. *Note:* This works only in certain locations, such as when displaying a web page in the Silk browser. Double-tapping in some other locations, such as when reading a book or viewing a video, will display tools.

✔ Place your fingers apart on a screen and pinch them together to zoom out on the current view; place your fingers together on the screen and then move them apart (unpinch) to enlarge the view.

Shop Now button

Unlock button

Figure 2-5: Swipe the Lock button to go to the Home screen.

✔ Swipe left to move to the next page in apps such as the e-reader or the Silk web browser. Swipe to the right to move to the previous page.

✔ Swipe up and down to scroll up and down a web page.

These touchscreen gestures will help you get around most of the content and setup screens you encounter in Kindle Fire HD.

Setting up your Kindle Fire HD

When you turn Kindle Fire HD on for the first time, you see a series of screens that help you set up and register the device. Don't worry: There aren't many questions, and you know all the answers.

At some point during this setup procedure, you may be prompted to plug your adapter in, if your battery charge is low. You may also be notified that the latest Kindle software is downloading and have to wait for that process to complete before you can move forward.

This is the point in the setup process at which you connect to a Wi-Fi network. You need this connection to register your device (if Amazon hasn't already pre-registered your device to your account). Follow these steps to register and set up your Kindle Fire HD:

1. **In the Connect to a Network list (shown on the screen in Figure 2-6), tap an available network.**

   Kindle Fire HD connects to the network (you may need to enter a password and then tap Connect to access an available network).

2. **On the Register Your Kindle screen that appears (see Figure 2-7), enter your Amazon account information, e-mail address, and a password in the appropriate fields, and then skip to Step 5; if you don't have an Amazon account, see Step 3.**

   You can choose to deselect the Show Password check box so that your password doesn't appear on your screen as you type it. This protects your password from prying eyes.

3. **If you don't have an Amazon account, click the New to Amazon? Create Account link.**

   This link takes you to the Create an Amazon Account screen (see Figure 2-8), with fields for entering your name, e-mail address, and password (which you have to retype to confirm).

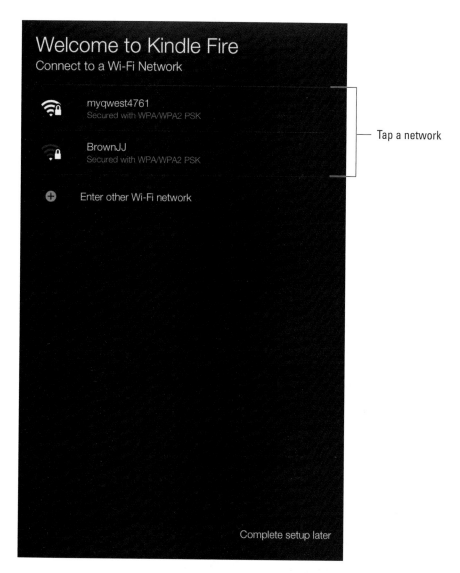

Figure 2-6: Start by connecting to a Wi-Fi network.

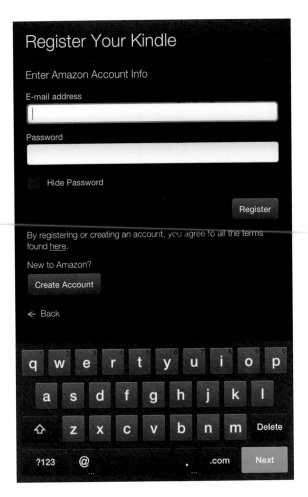

Figure 2-7: Register your Kindle Fire HD to use it.

4. **Enter this information, and then tap Continue.**

5. **If you want to read the terms of registration, tap the By Registering, You Agree to All of the Terms Found Here link.**

6. **When you finish reading the terms, tap the Close button to return to the registration screen.**

7. **To complete the registration with an existing or new account, tap the Register button.**

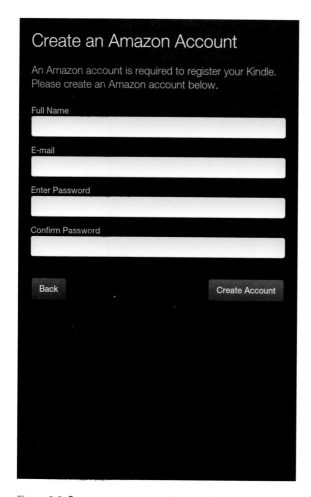

Figure 2-8: Create a new account by entering a few details.

8. **Tap to select a time zone from the list provided (see Figure 2-9) and then tap Continue.**

   For countries other than the United States, tap More and choose from the provided list. After you select from the list, tap the Back button in the bottom-left corner to return to the Time Zone screen.

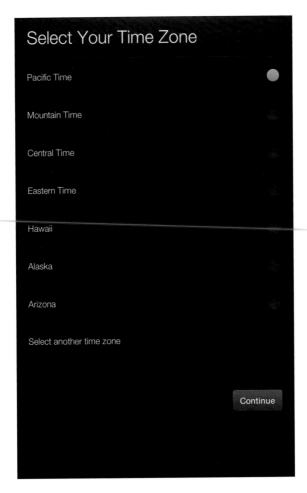

Figure 2-9: Choose the appropriate time zone from this list.

9. **A final screen appears asking you to confirm your account. Tap Continue.**

There's also a link labeled Not *<Your Name>*? If, for some reason, you aren't you (for example, you may have entered your account information incorrectly), tap the Not *<Your Name>* link to change your account information and then return to this screen.

10. **The next screen, labeled Connect Social Networks (see Figure 2-10), shows what social networks, if any, you're connected to.**

    These connections are a result of connections you may have to your Amazon account. If there are accounts here labeled, for example, Connect Your Twitter Account, you can tap them to connect.

11. **To proceed, tap Get Started Now.**

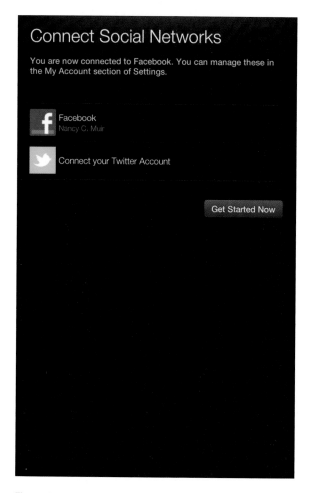

Figure 2-10: If you want to connect to your Facebook or Twitter accounts, tap each here.

At this point you see the first of several screens that acquaint you with the features of Kindle Fire HD and how to use some of the major ones. Tap the Next button on the middle-right side of these screens (see Figure 2-11) to proceed through the brief tutorial. At the end of the series, tap the Close button to go to the Kindle Fire HD Home screen. If you need more help at any time, you can refer to the User's Guide in the Kindle Fire HD Docs library.

You can also register an account at a later time by swiping down on the status bar at the top of the Home screen to display the Quick Settings, tapping More, and then tapping My Account. Tap the Register button on the next screen and enter your account information.

Figure 2-11: This very quick tutorial covers the basics of using Kindle Fire HD.

When you register your Kindle Fire HD to your Amazon account, a Kindle Fire e-mail address is created. You can use this e-mail address to send or have other people send documents to you that then appear in your Docs library on your Kindle Fire HD. See Chapter 10 for more about working with Docs.

Charging the battery

According to various media sources that have benchmarked Kindle Fire HD's performance, it has a battery life of about eight hours for Wi-Fi–connected activities, such as web browsing, streaming movies, and listening to music from the Cloud. If you're a bookworm who's more into the printed word than media, you'll be happy to hear that Amazon claims you get about 11 hours of reading downloaded books with Wi-Fi turned off.

You charge the battery by using the provided Micro USB cable plus a power adapter you'll have to supply yourself. Attach the smaller end of the Micro USB cable to your Kindle Fire HD's Micro USB port, located along the right side of the device when held in portrait orientation (refer to Figure 2-2), and the other end of the Micro USB cable into the power adapter, which you then plug into a wall outlet. If Kindle Fire HD is completely out of juice, it will take about four hours to charge it.

There's a battery indicator on the Status bar that runs across the top of the Kindle Fire HD screen that you can check to see if your battery is running low. The more green in the little battery icon, the more battery time you have left.

Getting to Know the Interface

The interface you see on the Kindle Home screen (see Figure 2-12) is made up of four items. At the top is a Search field which allows you to search all of your content and apps. Next, you see a set of buttons that take you to the Kindle Fire HD libraries that contain various types of content. In the middle of the screen is the Carousel. The Carousel contains images of items you recently used that you can flick with your finger to scroll through and tap any item to open it. Finally, the bottom portion of the Home screen contains a Customers Also Bought listing of other items that Amazon imagines you might enjoy based on your other purchases.

If the item foremost on your Carousel is a movie, you may see an X-Ray item on the far left of the Customers Also Bought listing as you do in Figure 2-12. X-Ray is an informational service based on the IMDb movie database that provides some background information about movie casts and crew. See Chapter 8 for more about this feature.

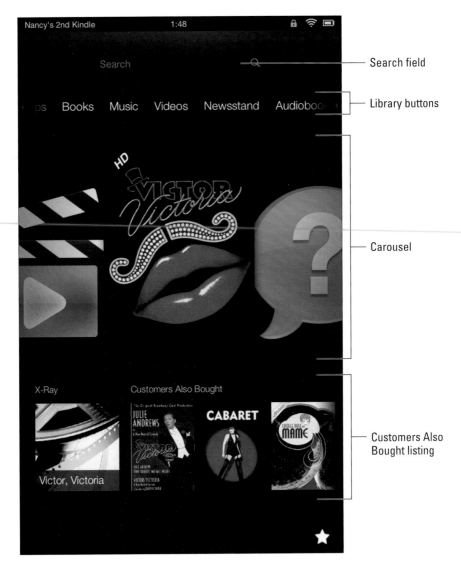

Search field

Library buttons

Carousel

Customers Also
Bought listing

Figure 2-12: This graphical interface is fun to move around with the flick of a finger.

Understanding the Cloud and Kindle Fire HD

Everything you buy using Kindle Fire HD's features is purchased through Amazon or its affiliates on the Amazon site. That content is downloaded to your device through a technology called Whispersync, which requires a Wi-Fi connection unless you have the Kindle Fire HD 4G LTE Wireless model.

When you purchase content, you can choose whether to keep it in the Amazon Cloud or download it to your Kindle Fire HD. If you download it, you can access it whether or not you're in range of a Wi-Fi network. At any time, you can remove content from the device, and it will be archived in the Cloud for you to stream to your device (music or video) or re-download (music, video, books, and magazines) anytime you like. Keeping content you're not currently using in the Amazon Cloud can save space on your device.

Accessing Kindle Fire HD libraries

Kindle Fire HD libraries are where you access downloaded content, as well as content stored by Amazon in the Cloud. Libraries (with the exception of the Docs library) also offer a Store button that you can tap to go online to browse and buy more content.

Tap any library button to open a library of downloaded and archived content: Games, Apps, Books, Music, Videos, Newsstand, Audiobooks, or Photos. Note that there's also a Docs button, where documents that you sideload from your computer or receive as e-mail attachments in your Kindle inbox are placed, as well as a Shop button to take you directly to Amazon Stores, and an Offers button where you can find Amazon special offers.

The Videos button opens to the Amazon store rather than a library because in most cases, it's not very prudent to download video content to your Kindle Fire HD. Because this type of content takes up so much of your device's memory, it's preferable to play video from Amazon's Cloud (which is called *streaming*).

There's also a Web button in among the list of libraries that you can tap to open the Silk web browser. Find out more about going online and using the browser in Chapter 5.

In a library, such as the Music library shown in Figure 2-13, you can tap the Device or Cloud tab located in the top-middle of the screen. The Device tab shows you only content you have downloaded; the Cloud tab displays all your purchases or free content stored in Amazon's Cloud library, including content you've downloaded to the Kindle Fire HD.

You can download archived content to your device at any time or remove downloaded content to the Cloud. You can also view the contents of libraries in different ways, depending on which library you're in. For example, you can view Music library contents by categories such as Songs, Artists, and Albums.

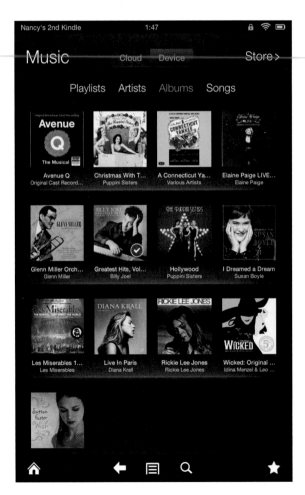

Figure 2-13: Your Music library provides access to all your musical content.

See Chapter 4 for more about buying content, Chapter 6 for information about reading books and magazines, and Chapters 7 and 8 for more about playing music and video.

It's possible to download video, which is useful if you'll be out of range of a Wi-Fi connection, but I recommend you remove the content from your device when you're done watching and back in Wi-Fi range. Removing content from Kindle Fire HD involves pressing it with your finger and choosing Remove from Device from the menu that appears.

As mentioned before, you can also sideload content you've obtained from other sources, such as iTunes, to your Kindle Fire HD libraries. Sideloading involves connecting the Micro USB cable that came with your Kindle Fire HD to your computer, and then copying content to Kindle Fire HD. See the section "Using a Micro USB Cable to Transfer Data," later in this chapter, for more about this process.

Playing with the Carousel

Many of us have fond memories of riding a carousel at the fair as kids. The Kindle Fire HD Carousel may not bring the same thrill, but it does have its charms as you swipe through it to see a revolving display of recently used books, audiobooks, music, videos, websites, docs, and apps (see Figure 2-14).

If you've used an Android device, such as a smartphone, you've probably encountered the Carousel concept. On Kindle Fire HD, items you've used recently are displayed here chronologically, with the most recent item you used on top. You can swipe your finger to the right or left to flick through the Carousel contents. When you find an item you want to view or play, tap to open it.

Whatever you tap opens in the associated player or reader. Music will open in the Amazon MP3 music player; video in the Amazon Video player; and docs, books, and magazines in the Kindle e-reader.

When you first begin using Kindle Fire HD, before you've accessed any content, by default the Carousel contains the Amazon Kindle User Guide and the absolutely free *New Oxford American Dictionary*. It may also contain recently used content from your Amazon Cloud library.

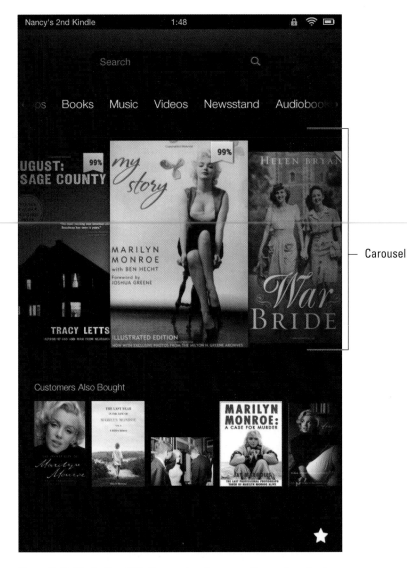

Figure 2-14: Kindle Fire HD's Carousel makes recently used content available.

Organizing Favorites

When you're on a roll using Kindle Fire HD for accessing all kinds of content, the Carousel can get a bit crowded. You may have to swipe five or six times to find what you need. That's where Favorites comes in.

The concept of Favorites is probably familiar to you from working with web browsers, in which Favorites is a feature that allows you to put websites you visit frequently in a Favorites folder. On the Kindle Fire HD, Favorites is also a place for saving frequently used content which takes the form of a pop-up display.

If, for example, you're reading a book you open often or you play a certain piece of music frequently, place it in the Favorites area of the Kindle Fire HD, and you can find it more quickly.

By default, Favorites includes the Silk browser, the E-mail app, Help & Support, and the IMDb movie database app. To pin an item to Favorites, press and hold it in the Carousel or a library, and then tap Add to Favorites from the menu that appears (see Figure 2-15).

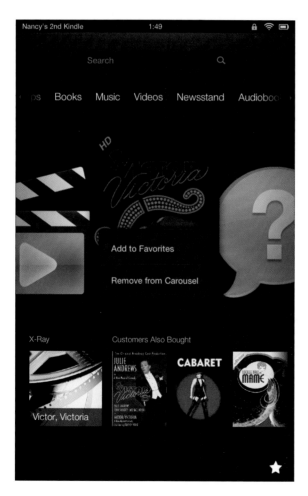

Figure 2-15: Pin items to Favorites by using this menu.

To remove content from Favorites, tap the Favorites button (the star in the bottom-left corner of the screen; refer to Figure 2-3) and, in the list of Favorites that appears, press and hold the item you want to remove and then tap Remove from Favorites from the menu that appears (see Figure 2-16). Remove from Favorites unpins the item from Favorites, although it's still available to you on the Carousel and in the related library. Delete removes the item from the device (although it's still archived in Amazon's Cloud).

Figure 2-16: Use this menu to manage Favorites.

Getting clues from the Status bar

The Status bar runs across the top of every Kindle Fire HD screen, just like the Status bar on your mobile phone. This bar, shown in Figure 2-17, provides information about the time, your network connection, and your battery charge; it also provides access to the Kindle Fire HD settings.

Nancy's 2nd Kindle   1:50

Figure 2-17: The various tools and settings available on the Status bar.

Here's a rundown of what you'll find on the Status bar:

- **Device name:** First is the name of your Kindle Fire HD, such as Nancy's Kindle or Nancy's 2nd Kindle.

- **Notifications:** A number sometimes appears just to the right of the device name to indicate that you have that many Notifications. Notifications can come from the Kindle Fire HD system announcing a completed download or the e-mail client announcing that a new e-mail has arrived, for example. To view all your notifications, swipe down from the Status bar, and a list appears (see Figure 2-18).

- **Current time:** The item in the middle of the Status bar is the current time, based on the time zone you specified when setting up the Kindle Fire HD.

- **Wireless:** The item on the Status bar to the right of the time is an icon showing you the Wi-Fi connection status. If this is lit up, you're connected. The more bars in the symbol that are bright white, the stronger the connection.

- **Bluetooth:** This icon appears when Bluetooth is turned on and displays in a blue color when another Bluetooth device is connected.

- **Battery charge:** Finally, the battery icon on the far-right side of the Status bar indicates the percentage of charge remaining on your battery.

Figure 2-18: The list of current notifications that you can display from any screen.

You can swipe down on the Status bar to access Quick Settings. Quick Settings (see Figure 2-19) offer the most commonly used settings. Use these items to adjust volume, brightness, or your Wi-Fi connection, for example. To access the full Kindle Fire HD Settings menu, tap More on the right of the Quick Settings bar. See Chapter 3 for a detailed breakdown of all Kindle Fire HD settings.

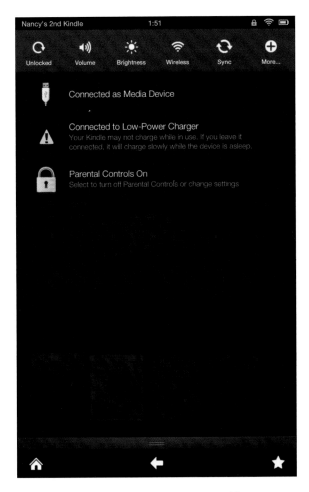

Figure 2-19: Use the Quick Settings menu or tap More to access the full complement of settings for Kindle Fire HD.

The often-present, ever-changing Options bar

The Options bar runs along the bottom or right side of your Kindle Fire HD screen, depending on which app or library you open. In some apps the Options bar is always visible; if the Options bar is hidden you will typically see a small black tab with lines on it either on the right side or bottom of the screen which you can swipe to display the Options bar. In other cases (as in the e-reader app) just tap on the screen and the Options bar appears.

The items offered on the Options bar change, depending on what library or app you're using, but they always include a Home button. Also, there are often items such as Search to run a search in features such as a content library and a Favorites button for adding an item to Favorites. In addition, you'll often see a Menu button when you tap the Options bar. This icon, which looks like a little box with three lines in it, makes available commonly used settings for the currently displayed feature. Figure 2-20 shows you the options available on the Newsstand library screen.

Figure 2-20: The Options bar offers contextually relevant options, depending on which app is displayed.

Use the Home button to jump back to the Kindle Fire HD Home screen from anywhere. On some screens where it would be annoying to be distracted by the Options bar, such as the e-reader, you may have to tap the screen to make the Options bar appear.

Using a Micro USB Cable to Transfer Data

It's easy to purchase or rent content from Amazon, which you can choose to download directly to your Kindle Fire HD or stream from the Amazon Cloud. However, you may want to get content from other places, such as iTunes or your Pictures folder on your computer, and play or view it on your Kindle Fire HD.

To transfer content to Kindle Fire HD, you have to use the Micro USB cable that came with your Kindle Fire HD. This cable has a USB connector on one end that you can plug into your PC or Mac, and a Micro USB connector on the other that fits into the Micro USB port on your Kindle Fire HD (which is located on the right side when holding Kindle Fire HD in portrait orientation; refer to Figure 2-2).

Attach the Micro USB end to your Kindle Fire HD (see Figure 2-21) and the USB end to your computer. Your Kindle Fire HD should then appear as a drive in Windows Explorer (see Figure 2-22) or the Mac Finder. You can now click and drag files from your hard drive to the Kindle Fire HD or use the copy and paste functions to accomplish the same thing.

Figure 2-21: Connecting the Micro USB cable to Kindle Fire HD.

Using this process, you can transfer apps, photos, docs, music, e-books, and videos from your computer to your Kindle Fire HD. Then, just tap the relevant library (such as Books for e-books and Music for songs) to read or play the content on your Kindle Fire HD.

You can also upload content to your Amazon Cloud Drive on your computer, and that content will then be available on your Kindle Fire HD.

Figure 2-22: Kindle Fire HD contents shown as a drive in Windows Explorer.

3

Kindle Fire HD Settings

*W*hen you first take your Kindle Fire HD out of the box, Amazon has provided you with default settings that will work for most people most of the time. However, we've all gotten used to being able to personalize our experience with phone and computer devices, so you may be curious about the various ways in which you can make Kindle Fire HD work uniquely for you.

On a tablet device such as Kindle Fire HD, there are dozens of settings that help you manage your tablet experience. Some of these settings are discussed in the chapters that cover individual apps, such as the Amazon video player (Chapter 8) and Contacts (Chapter 9). But other settings you may need to review when you start using your Kindle Fire HD; I cover those more general settings in this chapter.

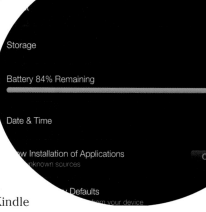

Opening Quick Settings

In this fast-paced day and age, quick is the name of the game for most of us, so Amazon has provided you with Quick Settings to streamline your settings experience.

You access both a short list of commonly used settings (Quick Settings) and all the more detailed settings for Kindle Fire HD by swiping downward from the top of the screen.

Here are the settings that you can control from the Quick Settings menu (see Figure 3-1):

Figure 3-1: Quick Settings control the settings that you access most often.

✓ **Unlocked/Locked:** This is a toggle feature, meaning that you tap it to lock your device so that the screen won't dim after a period of time, and tap it again to allow it to dim, which can save your battery power. Locked is a useful setting when you're reading a book or watching a movie, for example.

✓ **Volume:** Tap Volume to display a slider bar that you can use to increase (by sliding it to the right) or decrease (by sliding it to the left) the volume (see Figure 3-2).

Figure 3-2: Controls that appear when you tap Volume.

- **Brightness:** You can tap and display the Automatic Brightness On/Off button to turn on or off a feature that controls the brightness of the screen based on ambient light. You can also use the slider above this setting (see Figure 3-3) to adjust the brightness manually.

- **Wireless:** Tap to display the Airplane Mode On/Off button (see Figure 3-4); with Airplane Mode set to On, no available networks appear. When you set Airplane Mode to Off, a list of available networks appears. Tap an available network to join it. Note that you may be asked to enter a password to access some networks. For more on Wireless settings, see the section "Setting up Wi-Fi," later in this chapter.

Figure 3-3: Adjust brightness manually by using this slider.

✔ **Sync:** Generally speaking, if you're within range of a Wi-Fi network, when you begin to download content it downloads very quickly. However, if you've been out of range of a network, you might want to use this setting when you're back in range of a network to manually initiate the download of new content or continue downloads that may have been interrupted.

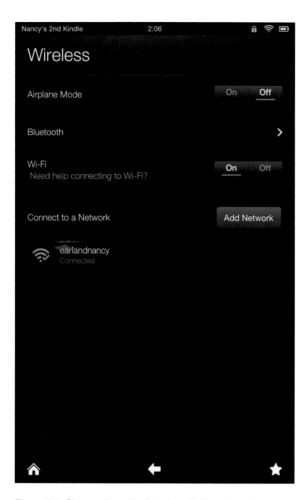

Figure 3-4: Choose from the list of available networks.

Finding Other Settings

Beyond what I discuss in the preceding section, there's one more item on the Quick Settings menu — More. Figure 3-5 shows you the many settings that appear when you tap the More button.

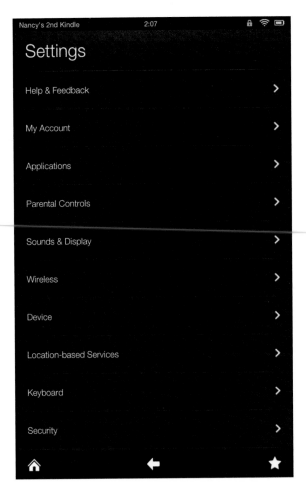

Figure 3-5: Plenty more settings are revealed when you tap More.

These settings include: Help & Feedback, My Account, Applications, Parental Controls, Sounds & Display, Wireless, Device, Location-Based Services, Keyboard, Security, and Legal & Compliance.

You won't need to change many of these settings very often because the way Kindle Fire HD works out of the box is usually very intuitive. But if you do find that you want to make an adjustment to settings such as the date and time or parental controls, it's useful to know what's available.

The following sections give you the skinny on what settings appear when you tap More in the Quick Settings menu.

Help & Feedback

Now and then, we all need a bit of help, and when you're first using a new device such as Kindle Fire HD, you should know where to find that help (on the off chance you don't have this book handy).

When you tap More from Quick Settings and then tap Help & Feedback, you see the Help & Feedback screen (see Figure 3-6), which offers a world of help and allows you to interact with Amazon customer service.

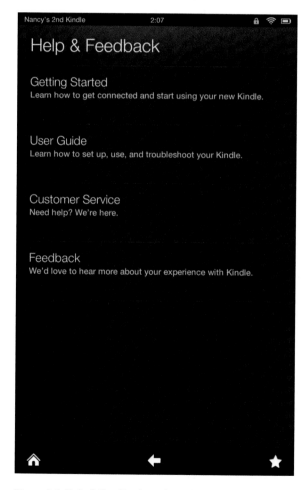

Figure 3-6: Help & Feedback settings for Kindle Fire HD.

The Help & Feedback screen includes four somewhat self-explanatory items: Getting Started, User Guide, Customer Service, and Feedback. The last two items display a form in which you can type a message to send on to Amazon. Here's how all four Help & Feedback options work:

- **Getting Started:** Use this feature to get help with the following topics: Your Kindle at a Glance; Connecting Wirelessly; Set Up Your Kindle; and Kindle Support Pages.
- **User Guide:** The User Guide (see Figure 3-7) offers more comprehensive help on a few dozen topics such as Navigation, Shop, Games, Web, and Video Chat.

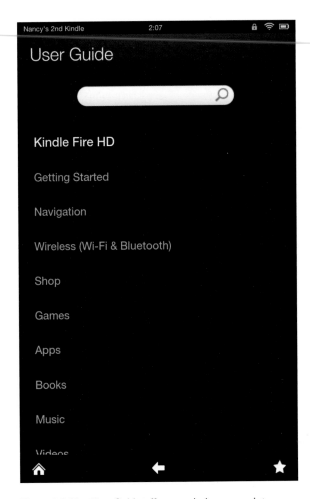

Figure 3-7: The User Guide offers you help on a variety of topics.

✔ **Customer Service:** The first question you have to answer here is "What can we help you with?" Tap the Select an Issue drop-down list to locate your issue and then tap that issue to select it. You can then tap the Select Issue Details drop-down list that appears to choose a more specific topic. Choose from the How Would You Like to Contact Us options by tapping either the E-Mail or Phone button.

✔ **Feedback:** Tap Select a Feature and choose from the list that appears (items such as Newsstand, Books, Docs, and so on). Then, tap Back to go back to Feedback. Enter your comment in the Tell Us What You Think about This Feature field (see Figure 3-8). You can also tap one to five stars to rate the feature you're providing feedback on. Tap the Send Feedback button to submit your thoughts to Amazon.

My Account

Kindle Fire HD does much of what it does by accessing your Amazon account. You need to have an Amazon account to shop, access the Amazon Cloud Drive library online, and register your Kindle Fire HD, for example.

The My Account option in Settings provides information about the account to which the device is registered (see Figure 3-9). To view your Kindle e-mail address, tap the Learn More About Your Kindle Email Address link. To remove this account from your Kindle Fire HD, from the My Account screen you can tap the Deregister button. Because the obvious thing to do next is to register your Kindle Fire HD to another account (because so much depends on your having an associated account), you then are presented with a Register button. Tap Register and fill in your Amazon username and password to register the device.

If you deregister your account, don't register your Kindle Fire HD, and leave this screen, you're placed in the introductory demo that appeared when you first set up your Kindle Fire HD. When you finish that demo and tap any category, such as Books, you're again prompted to register your device to your Amazon account.

The My Account screen also offers the option of managing social networking accounts and e-mail accounts. Tap the Manage Social Network Accounts link to set up your Twitter and/or Facebook account so that you can take advantage of built-in features for sharing information via either service. Tap the Manage E-Mail Accounts link to manage general e-mail settings, such as whether attachments should be downloaded automatically and whether contacts and calendar entries should be synced from your e-mail account to Kindle Fire HD. You can also use a setting to add a different e-mail account. (The e-mail account set up automatically for you is the one you have associated with your Amazon account.)

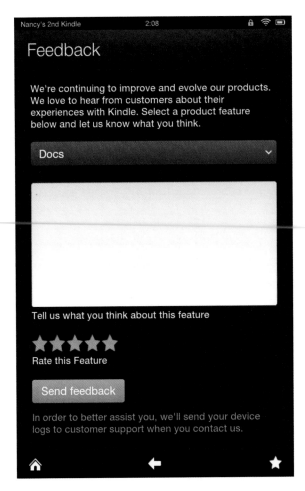

Figure 3-8: The Feedback feature of Help & Feedback gives you the ability to rate features of Kindle Fire HD and provide comments.

Parental Controls

When you tap the Parental Controls setting, you're first presented with the option of turning the controls on. Tap to turn them on, enter and confirm a password, and then tap Finish.

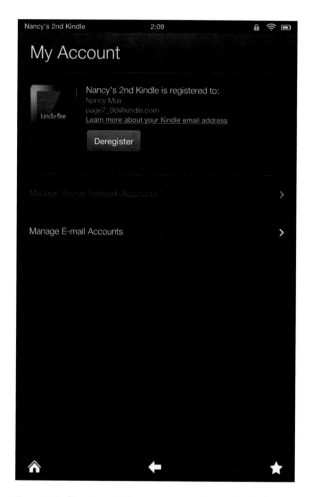

Figure 3-9: Check which Amazon account your device is registered to.

In the following screen (see Figure 3-10), tap to unblock the Web Browser or E-Mail, Contacts, and Calendars settings. You can also tap to password protect purchases or video playback. If you want to allow or block certain types of content, tap Block and Unblock Content Types and then tap the content you want to block, such as Music, Video, or Apps and Games.

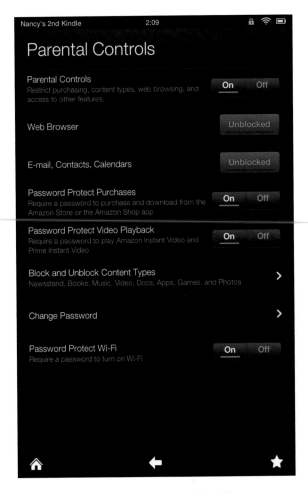

Figure 3-10: Choose what to block or unblock here.

Finally, you can tap to turn on or off the Password Protect Wi-Fi feature. When this feature is on, anybody using your Kindle Fire HD has to enter a password to make an online connection.

Controlling sounds and display

With a tablet that's so media-centric, accessing music and video, as well as games that you can play with their accompanying screeches and sounds, it's important that you know how to control the volume.

If you tap Sounds & Display in Settings (see Figure 3-11), you see a volume slider that you can use to increase or decrease the volume, as well as a setting for turning Dolby Digital Plus on or off. The Dolby setting improves Kindle Fire HD's sound quality but may use up more of your battery life.

You also see two settings controlling the sounds for notifications: Mute All Notifications and Notification Sounds. Notifications may come from the arrival of a new e-mail, a completed download, or an app notification (such as an appointment reminder from a calendar app that you may have downloaded). To modify notification sounds, tap Mute All Notifications to (you guessed it) mute sounds for notifications, or tap the arrow to the right of the Notification Sounds option and, from the list that appears, choose the sound you want to use.

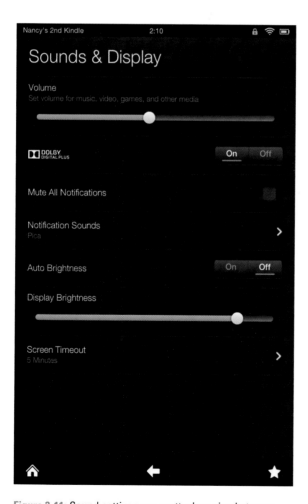

Figure 3-11: Sound settings are pretty darn simple to use.

Sounds & Display also allows you to manage your device's display, adjusting both the screen brightness and how long it takes for the screen to lock when the device isn't being used, a feature called Screen Timeout.

On the Settings screen, tap Sounds & Display to begin to work with these settings (refer to Figure 3-11):

- **Auto Brightness:** Turn this feature on to have Kindle Fire HD adjust its screen brightness based on available light.

- **Display Brightness:** Tap and drag the circle on this slider to the right to make the screen brighter and to the left to dim it.

- **Screen Timeout:** After a certain period of inactivity, the Kindle Fire HD screen will lock and go black to save battery power. You can adjust the length of this interval by tapping the arrow in this field and choosing from a list that ranges from 30 seconds to one hour. You can also choose the option Never if you want your screen to be always on. However, remember that using the Never option for a very long interval will wear down your battery.

Location-Based Services

New with Kindle Fire HD is a location-based feature that enables the device to know where you are in the world. This is useful for some apps and Kindle Fire HD features that need to know where you are in order to provide information or services such as weather or local traffic reports. When an app or website is using your location information, you'll see an icon that looks like a cross in a circle in the upper-right corner of the screen near your battery life icon.

To turn location-based services on or off, in Settings, tap Location-Based Services and then tap the On/Off button.

If you turn location-based services on, you're sharing very private information about your whereabouts. If you're concerned about what apps have access to your location, check out those apps in the Amazon Appstore to see whether the permissions listed on their details page mention use of location information.

Making security settings

The first thing you can do to keep your Kindle Fire HD secure is to never let it out of your hands. But because we can't control everything and sometimes things get lost or stolen, it's a good idea to assign a password that's required to unlock your Kindle Fire HD screen. If other people get their hands on your Kindle Fire HD, there's no way they can get at stored data, such as your Amazon account information or contacts, without knowing the password.

In Settings, tap the Security option and you'll see five simple choices (see Figure 3-12):

- **Lock Screen Password:** Simply tap the On button to require that a password be used to unlock your device. When you do, fields appear labeled Enter Password and Confirm Password. Tap in the Enter Password field and, using the onscreen keyboard that appears, type a password. Tap in the Confirm Password field and retype the password. Tap Finish to save your new password.

- **Credential Storage:** Credentials are typically used for Microsoft Exchange–based accounts, such as an account you use to access e-mail on your company's server. If you use Microsoft Exchange, it's a good idea to get your network administrator's help to make the following settings: Install Secure Credentials, Set Credential Storage Password, Use Secure Credentials, and Clear Credential Storage.

- **VPN:** If you want to use Kindle Fire HD on a virtual private network (a network that allows you to connect to a remote network), you have to use this feature to first download a VPN app. As with Credential Storage, if you want to use VPN, it's a good idea to get your network administrator's help with this feature.

- **Device Administrators:** If your device is being administered through a company Exchange account, use this setting to establish the device administrator who can modify settings for the account.

- **Enable ADB:** This setting allows those developing apps for Kindle Fire HD to run debugging programs using a USB connection; the average Kindle Fire HD user doesn't need to worry about using this feature.

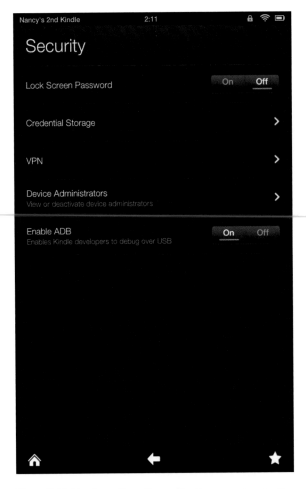

Figure 3-12: The Security settings offer five ways to secure your Kindle Fire HD.

Working with applications

Apps can help you do everything from manage e-mail to play games. Managing the way apps work on your Kindle Fire HD is done through the Applications setting.

You access the Applications setting by tapping Applications on the Setting screen (refer to Figure 3-5). The Applications screen (see Figure 3-13) provides you with a list of installed apps, including the app that controls Notification settings.

Tap Installed Applications and then tap on any of the installed apps, such as Calendar or Amazon Kindle, and you encounter the following options:

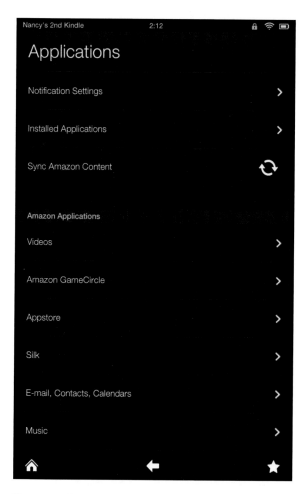

Figure 3-13: Each application on your Kindle Fire HD has associated settings.

- ✔ **Force Stop:** Force Stop allows Kindle Fire HD to stop an application from running if it encounters problems.

- ✔ **Storage:** You can clear Kindle Fire HD's memory of data stored by the app by tapping the Clear Data button.

- ✔ **Cache:** Computing devices store data based on your usage to more quickly provide the data you need. This so-called cache of data fills up a bit of memory, so if you want to free up some memory, tap the Clear Cache button.

- ✔ **Launch by Default:** Tap this button to launch an app automatically when you turn on Kindle Fire HD, if that option is available.

- ✔ **Permissions:** A list of permissions to allow access to information that this app might have to use to perform its function, such as your location.

Adjusting date and time

You chose a Time Zone setting when you first set up your Kindle Fire HD (see Chapter 2). Your Kindle Fire HD uses the Date & Time setting to display the correct time in the Status bar, and also to work with other apps, such as a third-party calendar app, for example. Tap Device in the Settings screen, and then tap Date & Time to see the four options shown in Figure 3-14:

- ✔ **Time:** This setting is controlled by which time zone you select.

- ✔ **Date:** This setting is also controlled by which time zone you select.

- ✔ **Select Time Zone:** Tap the arrow to the right of this setting to change your time zone and then tap to the right side of the time zone you want to use (see Figure 3-15).

- ✔ **Use 24-Hour Format:** If you want to use a 24-hour military-style clock, leave this setting on; if you'd rather use a 12-hour clock, tap to turn this setting off.

Setting up Wi-Fi

Wireless is a pretty essential setting for using Kindle Fire HD. Without a Wi-Fi connection, you can't stream video or music, shop at the various Amazon stores, or send and receive e-mail.

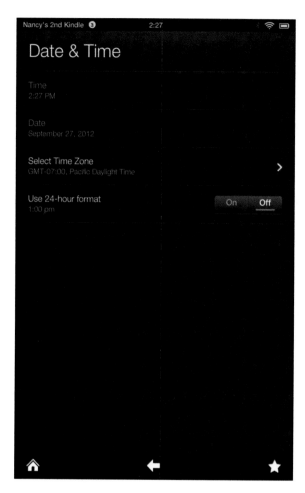

Figure 3-14: Let Kindle Fire HD control your time and date with the Time Zone setting.

Figure 3-15: Manually set the time zone on your Kindle Fire HD.

Tap Wireless in the Quick Settings screen to view the settings shown in Figure 3-16:

- ✓ **Airplane Mode:** Turn this setting on or off. With Airplane Mode on, you can't join a network.

- ✓ **Bluetooth:** Tap here to access Bluetooth settings that allow you to enable and connect to a Bluetooth device such as a Bluetooth printer or cellphone.

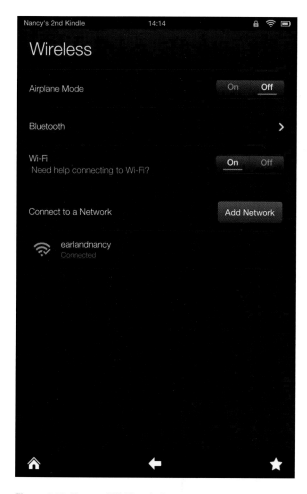

Figure 3-16: Turn on Wi-Fi and choose your preferred Wi-Fi network.

- **Wi-Fi:** Tap the On/Off button to turn Wi-Fi on or off. Note that turning Wi-Fi off may save some of your Kindle Fire HD's battery life.

- **Connect to a Network:** Tap any network listed under this heading to connect to it; if you're in range of a network that isn't listed here automatically, tap the Add Network button and enter the network's SSID (the public name of a Wi-Fi network) and security information to add it to the list of available networks and connect to it.

Working with the onscreen keyboard

There's no physical keyboard with your Kindle Fire HD, so you depend on its onscreen keyboard to provide input to apps such as OfficeSuite, or in fields used to search and enter text into forms, such as e-mail messages.

There are five simple things you can do when you choose Keyboard from the Settings list, three of which offer the basic On/Off choices (see Figure 3-17):

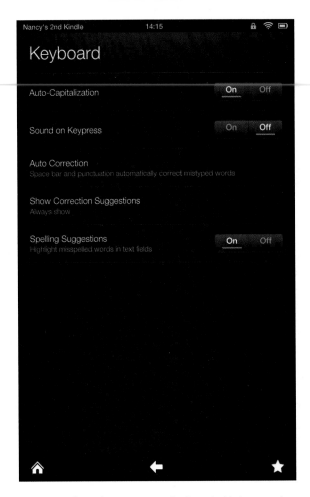

Figure 3-17: Control your onscreen keyboard with these settings.

- **Auto-Capitalization:** If you want Kindle Fire HD to automatically capitalize proper names or the first word in a sentence, tap to turn this setting on.

- **Sound on Keypress:** If you like that satisfying clicky sound when you tap a key on the onscreen keyboard, tap to turn this setting on.

- **Auto Correction:** Turning this setting on and choosing a correction level (such as Modest or Very Aggressive) allows Kindle Fire HD to correct common typing errors, such as typing *teh* when you mean *the*.

- **Show Correction Suggestions:** Tap this option and you can choose to always show correction suggestions, show them only when you're holding your Kindle Fire HD in portrait orientation (why? don't ask me), or always hide correction suggestions.

- **Spelling Suggestions:** If you turn this feature on, words in text fields that might be misspelled are highlighted.

Looking at device settings

You can check your Kindle Fire HD's Device settings (see Figure 3-18) to find out facts such as the remaining storage space available or your device's serial number. This is also where you can reset your Kindle Fire HD to the state it was in when it left the factory, if you like a clean slate now and then.

Here are the Device settings available to you:

- **About:** Here's where you can find the system version which relates to the operating system version for your Kindle Fire HD. New versions are released periodically, so if your version isn't the most current, you might need to update it by tapping the Update Your Kindle button (see Figure 3-19). You can also find your Kindle Fire HD's serial number (which you might need to reference when interacting with Amazon technical or customer support) and your Wi-Fi and Bluetooth MAC addresses in About.

- **Storage:** Tells you how much memory is still available on your device.

- **Battery:** Indicates the percentage of battery power remaining.

- **Date & Time:** Make settings for your time zone, as discussed in the section "Adjusting Date and Time," earlier in this chapter.

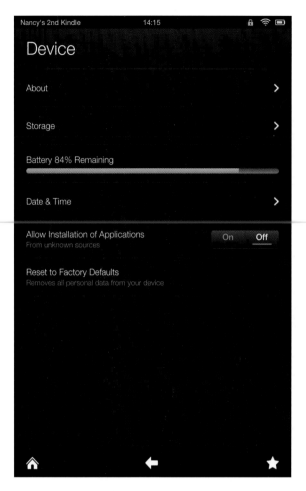

Figure 3-18: Device settings provide a lot of information about the status of your device.

✔ **Allow Installation of Applications:** Kindle Fire HD is set up to get its content from Amazon because they claim that provides some measure of confidence and security to customers. For example, apps you *sideload* (transfer) from your computer to Kindle Fire HD that are from third-party suppliers may introduce viruses to your device. If you want to allow porting of apps from other sources than Amazon, choose On for this setting. If you don't want to let apps other than those verified by Amazon to be placed on your Kindle Fire HD, tap Off.

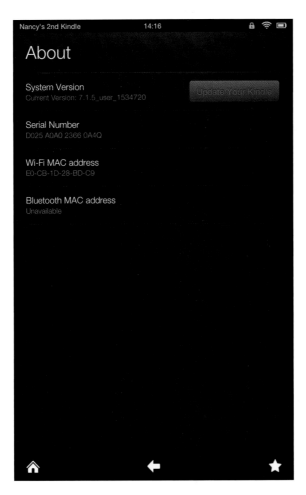

Figure 3-19: Amazon occasionally provides system updates; you can update manually.

✓ **Reset to Factory Defaults:** This setting could come in handy in a couple of situations. If you sell your Kindle Fire HD to somebody (so you can buy a newer version, of course!), you wouldn't want that person to have your docs and contact information. Also, if you've loaded a lot of content onto your Kindle Fire HD and then decide you want a clean beginning to clear up memory, you might choose to reset the device. Resetting wipes all content and any changes you've made to default settings. If you tap this setting, you see the confirming dialog box shown in Figure 3-20. Tap Erase Everything to continue with the reset procedure or Cancel to close the warning dialog box and halt the reset.

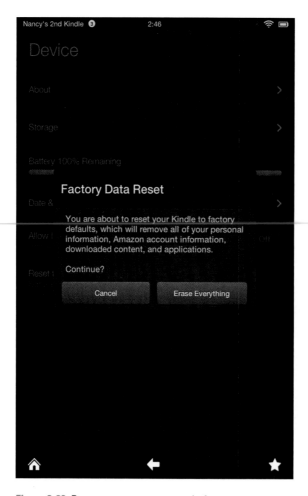

Figure 3-20: Be sure you want to reset before you accept this option.

Although you get a minimum of 16GB of storage with Kindle Fire HD, a chunk of that is taken up in pre-installed and system files. So the storage available may indicate that you have less total storage available on the device than you thought.

Part II
Taking the Leap Online

The 5th Wave   By Rich Tennant

"Hold on Barbara. I'm pretty sure there's an app for this."

In this part . . .

This part helps you buy apps and media content, such as music, videos, and magazines. You also explore how to go online and set up your e-mail account and Wi-Fi connection, and work with the Silk browser.

4

Going Shopping

In This Chapter

▷ Using your Amazon account

▷ Shopping at the Amazon Appstore

▷ Buying apps, music, video, and printed publications

▷ Buying other Amazon items through your Kindle Fire HD

*B*ecause Kindle Fire HD is, above all, a great device for consuming content (especially Amazon provided content), knowing how to buy that content or download free content is key to enjoying it. Amazon offers both a rich supply of books, magazines, music, and video, and an Amazon Appstore that you can use to get your hands on apps that add to the functionality of your Kindle Fire HD. These apps can range from simple accessories such as a notes program to fun and addictive games and maps programs.

In this chapter, you discover how to get apps as well as books, magazines, music, and videos for your Kindle Fire HD.

Managing Your Amazon Account

You buy things from Amazon by using the account and payment information you provide when you create an Amazon account. You probably have an account if you ever bought anything on Amazon (or opened an account when you bought your Kindle Fire HD). To buy things on Amazon with your Kindle Fire HD, you need to have associated your Amazon account with your Kindle Fire HD, which happens during the setup process, covered in Chapter 2, or which you can do by visiting the My Account section of Settings (see Figure 4-1). Swipe down on the top of your screen, tap More, and then choose My Account in the Settings page to view this screen.

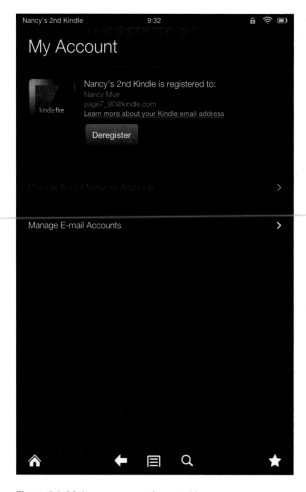

Figure 4-1: Make account settings at this screen.

After you associate your device with an Amazon account, you can manage account settings by following these steps:

1. **Navigate to the Amazon website (www.amazon.com) by using the browser on either your Kindle Fire HD or computer.**

2. **Tap (if you're using a touchscreen device) or click the Your Account option in the top-right corner of the Amazon screen (see Figure 4-2).**

3. **Tap or click the Manage Payment Options or Add a Credit or Debit Card option from the Payment section of your account.**

4. **Change or enter a new method of payment and billing address.**

You Account option

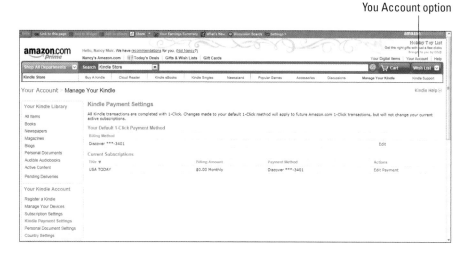

Figure 4-2: Managing your Amazon account on a PC.

Visiting the Amazon Appstore

After you create an Amazon account (which I discuss in the preceding section) you can start shopping for all kinds of content for your Kindle Fire HD. I'll start by introducing you to the world of apps.

Apps provide you with functionality of all kinds, from an app that turns your Kindle Fire HD into a star-gazing instrument to game apps. You can find acupuncture apps, drawing apps, and apps that provide maps so that you can find your way in the world.

Exploring the world of apps

You can buy apps for your Kindle Fire HD by using the Amazon Appstore. This store is full of apps written especially for devices that are based on the Android platform, including Kindle Fire HD.

Android devices may have slightly different operating systems, and therefore not every app will work on every device. See Chapters 11 and 12 for some suggested apps that will work well with your Kindle Fire HD.

Follow these steps to explore the world of apps:

1. **Tap the Apps button at the top of the Home screen to enter your Apps library.**

2. **Tap the Store button.**

   The store appears (see Figure 4-3).

Figure 4-3: The Amazon Appstore.

3. (Optional) At the top of the store is Today's Free App of the Day; tap this option to download a free app to your device.

You can get a different free app every day; just be sure you don't glut your Kindle Fire HD's memory with free apps you're not really going to use.

Tabs along the top of the Store include

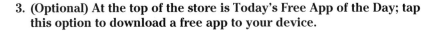 **Best Sellers:** This tab displays the best-selling apps in the store, including Top Paid, Top Free, and Top Rated Overall.

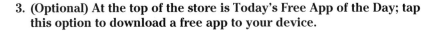 **Games:** Tap this tab to see featured game titles, as shown in Figure 4-4. Across the top of the Games section of the store are tabs such as Action, Arcade, Casual, Puzzles, and All Games.

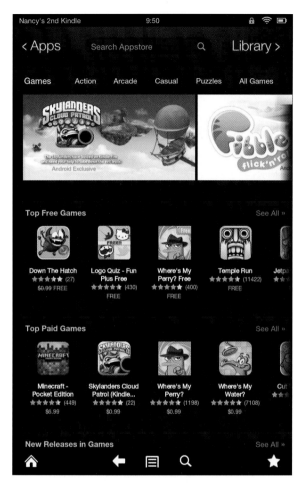

Figure 4-4: Games categories includes puzzles, action games, arcade games, and more.

✔ **New Releases:** Tap this tab to see recent releases across a variety of categories. This is a great way to browse what's been added since your last app shopping spree.

✔ **All Categories:** If you want to see all available categories, tap the All Categories tab to access categories ranging from Photography and Real Estate to Podcasts and Travel (see Figure 4-5).

For new releases related to your interests, scroll down the Appstore home page and view the Recommended for You and New for You list of apps you might enjoy based on your other app purchases.

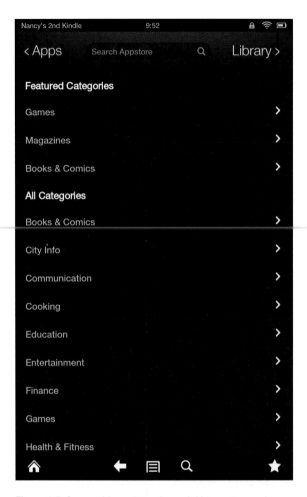

Figure 4-5: See a wide variety of special interest apps by tapping All Categories.

When you display a category of apps, note that you can tap the Refine button to sort the apps by several criteria such as Release Date or Price Low to High in the Sort feature, New Releases, Average Customer Review, or Price.

Searching for apps

You can have fun browsing through categories of apps, but if you know which app you want to buy, using the Search feature can take you right to it.

To search for an app, follow these steps:

1. **Tap in the Search field on the Appstore main page.**

   The keyboard shown in Figure 4-6 appears.

2. **Using the onscreen keyboard, enter the name of an app, such as the game Angry Birds.**

   Suggestions appear beneath the Search field.

3. **Tap a suggestion to display the list of suggestions with more detailed results, as shown in Figure 4-7.**

Figure 4-6: Use the search field and onscreen keyboard in the Appstore to find what you want.

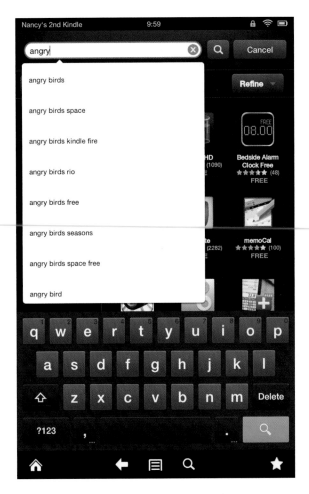

Figure 4-7: Search results in the Appstore.

4. Tap an app name to see more details about it.

The Product Info screen appears, as shown in Figure 4-8. Read the description and scroll down to read customer reviews or explore other apps that customers who bought this app also bought.

The Save for Later button adds the app to your Saved for Later list. You access this list by tapping the Menu button on the Options bar, tapping More, and then tapping Saved for Later. You can go to this list at any time to buy an item, or delete it from the list by pressing and holding your finger on it and then tapping Remove in the menu that appears.

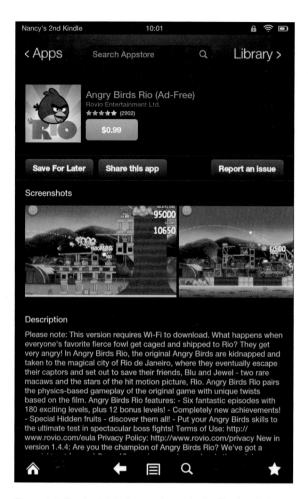

Figure 4-8: Product details are shown in the Product Info screen.

Buying apps

You might find something you want to own by browsing or searching, but however you find it, when you're ready to buy, you can follow these steps:

1. **From the app's Product Info screen (see the preceding section), tap the Price button.**

   Note that if the app is free, this button reads Free, but if you have to pay for the app, the app price (such as $0.99) is displayed on the button. When you tap the button, its label changes to Buy App (for paid apps) or Get App (for free apps). See Figure 4-9.

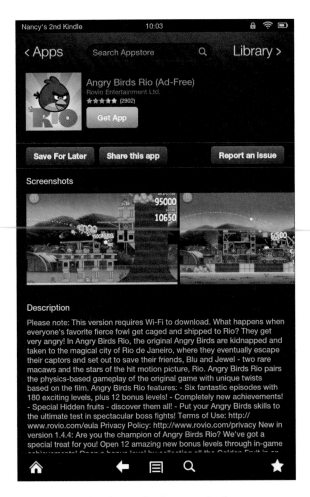

Figure 4-9: Tap Buy App or Get App to make the app your own.

2. **Tap the button again to download paid or free apps to your Kindle Fire HD.**

   A Downloading button appears, showing the download progress. When the installation is complete, an Open button appears.

3. **If you want to use the app immediately, tap the Open button.**

To use the app at any time, locate it in the App library or, if you've used it recently, on the Carousel; tap the app to open it. Each app has its own controls and settings, so look for a settings menu like the one for the Solitaire game shown in Figure 4-10.

Figure 4-10: App settings for Solitaire.

If you find an app that you like in the store, you can share it with others by using e-mail. Tap the Share This App button on the app description page in the Amazon Appstore (refer to Figure 4-8) to use this feature.

You can also buy apps from the Appstore on your PC or Mac. When placing the app in your shopping cart, be sure to select Kindle Fire HD for the device you want to download the app to in the drop-down list below the Add to Cart button. When you complete your purchase, assuming you're in range of a Wi-Fi network, the app is immediately downloaded to your Kindle Fire HD.

To delete an installed app from your App library, press and hold it until a menu appears and then tap Remove from Device. The app, however, isn't gone — it's still stored in the Amazon Cloud drive, and you can download it again at any time by tapping it in the Cloud tab of the App library.

Buying Content

Apps are great, but shopping for content is my favorite thing to do. I'm not putting down games and map apps, but to me, content means a night at the movies, a rainy afternoon with a good book, or a relaxing hour listening to a soothing collection of music.

From Amazon, you can buy publications, books, music, and video (movies and TV shows) to download or stream to your Kindle Fire HD. The buying process is somewhat similar for the different types of content, but there are slight variations, which I go into in the following sections.

Buying publications through Newsstand

There's a world of periodicals out there, from magazines to newspapers, just waiting for you to explore them. Kindle Fire HD's color display makes browsing through color magazines especially appealing.

Tap Newsstand on the Home page of Kindle Fire HD and then tap the Store button to see several categories of items (see Figure 4-11).

First, there are Featured Magazines with 30-day free trials displayed across the top. You can swipe right to left to scroll through these.

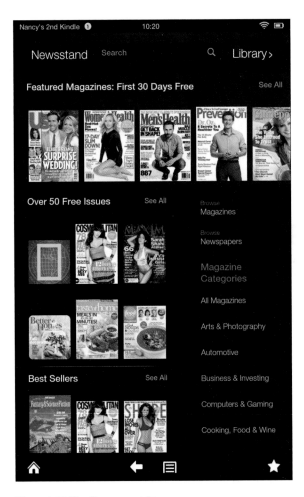

Figure 4-11: The Newsstand Store.

Below Free Trials, you see categories such as Best Sellers, Business & Investing, and Entertaining (though the categories might change on a regular basis). You can tap the See All button above any category to see a more complete list of included items.

When you find the publication you want, follow these steps to buy or subscribe to it:

1. **Tap the item.**

   A screen appears showing pricing, a description of the publication, and Subscribe Now and Buy Issue buttons (see Figure 4-12).

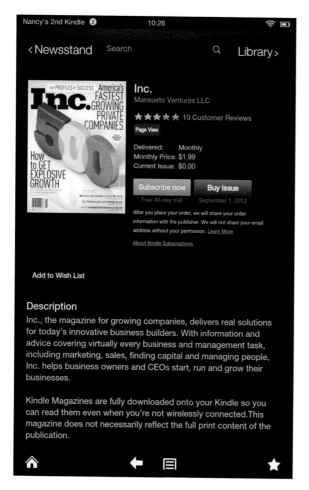

Figure 4-12: Details about a publication and buttons to help you purchase or subscribe.

2. **Tap Subscribe Now or Buy Issue.**

   The button label changes to read Downloading. During the download process you can tap the Cancel button if you change your mind. When the download is complete, the button label changes to Read Now.

3. **Tap the Read Now button to open the magazine.**

   Note that the magazine is stored in your Amazon Cloud library where you can read or download it to your Kindle Fire HD via Newsstand at a later time.

Buying books

I may be partial to books because I write them, but I hardly think I'm alone. If you've joined the electronic book revolution (or even if you haven't), you'll find that reading books on Kindle Fire HD is convenient and economical (e-books are typically a few dollars less than the print version, and you can borrow e-books from your local library for free).

To browse through e-books from Amazon on your Kindle Fire HD, follow these steps:

1. **Tap the Books button on the Kindle Fire HD Home screen.**

2. **Tap the Store button.**

   The Amazon Bookstore sports a Recommended for You section at the top which suggests books for you based on your buying history.

3. **Swipe right to left to scroll through the recommendations at the top.**

   You also see categories such as Kindle Select 25, Best Sellers, and Editor's Picks.

As with the Newsstand, when you locate and tap an item in the bookstore you see a screen with that item's pricing and description (see Figure 4-13). In the bookstore, the buttons you see at this point are labeled Try a Sample, Add to Wish List, and Buy (or Buy for Free). Here's how these three buttons work:

- **Try a Sample:** Tap this button, and it changes to a Downloading button, and then to a Read Now button. Tap the Read Now button to open the sample of the book.

- **Add to Wish List:** Tap to add the selection to your Wish List. You can view your Wish List at any time by tapping the Menu button on the Options bar and tapping Wish List.

- **Buy or Buy for Free:** Tap this button, and it changes to a Downloading button. When the download is complete, the button label changes to Read Now. Tap the Read Now button to open the book. Remember that the book is now stored in your Books library, where you can tap it to open and read it at your leisure.

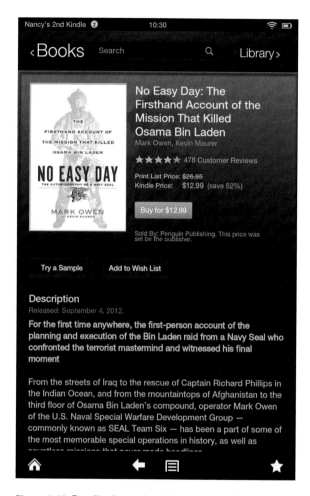

Figure 4-13: Details about a book in the Amazon Bookstore.

After you've read a bit of your new book, it will appear both in your Books library and on the Carousel on the Home screen.

To remove a book from your device (remembering that it will still be stored in the Amazon Cloud), open your Book library, press and hold the book, and tap Remove from Device from the menu that appears.

For more about reading e-books and periodicals on Kindle Fire, see Chapter 6.

Buying music

You may hate computer games, you might not read books very often, but I've never met anybody who doesn't like some kind of music. No matter what kind of music you prefer, from hip-hop to Broadway, you're likely to find a great many selections tucked away in Amazon's vaults.

Tap the Music button on the Kindle Fire HD Home screen and then tap the Store button. At the top-right of the Store screen, you see the following categories: Bestsellers, New Releases, and Genres. Tap one of these tabs to get a list of items in that category (see Figure 4-14). You can also tap categories such as New Releases and Recommended for You to view music by these criteria.

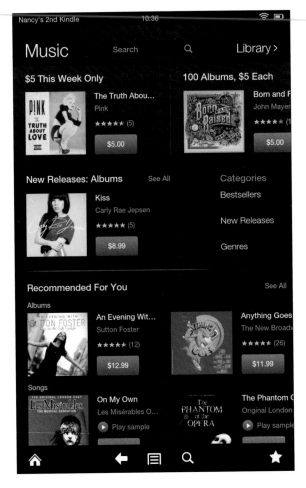

Figure 4-14: The Amazon Music Store.

All over the Music Store home page, you'll see thumbnails of music selections.

Follow these steps to buy music:

1. **Tap an item.**

   A screen appears, displaying a list of the songs in the case of an album with Price buttons for both the entire album and each individual song.

2. **Tap the arrow button to the left of a song to play a preview of it.**

3. **Tap a Price button.**

   The button label changes from the price of the item to the word Buy.

4. **Tap the Buy button.**

   The song or album downloads to your Music library. A confirmation dialog box opens, displaying a Go to Your Library button and a Continue Shopping button (see Figure 4-15).

5. **Tap the Go to Your Library button to open the album and display the list of songs.**

   The album is now stored both in your Music library and the Amazon Cloud Drive; if you tap on a song to play it, it'll also appear with recently accessed content in the Carousel. The first time you download music, you may be asked to choose whether you want content downloaded to your device when you buy it or stored in the Amazon Cloud drive.

   If you tap the Continue Shopping button, you can later find the album in your Music library.

See Chapter 7 for more about playing music.

Buying video

You should definitely check out the experience of consuming your video programs on a portable device such as Kindle Fire HD. From lying in bed or on the beach to watching your videos while waiting in line at the bank, portability can be a very convenient feature.

When you tap Videos on the Kindle Fire HD Home screen, you're instantly taken to the Amazon Video Store shown in Figure 4-16.

Across the top of the screen, you see thumbnails of items in the Prime Instant Videos category. Below these thumbnails is a horizontally scrolling list of thumbnails labeled Next Up that includes movies purchased. You can pick up where you left off viewing these items by tapping any of them.

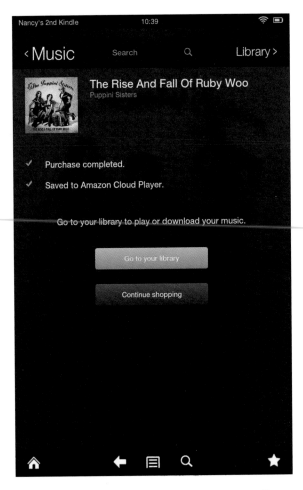

Figure 4-15: This dialog box allows you to return to your library or keep shopping.

Tap an item in the Prime Instant Video category, and a descriptive screen appears. For TV shows, this screen includes episode prices and a set of Season tabs. For movies, this screen may include Watch Trailer, Buy, and Rent buttons (see Figure 4-17). You can also scroll down and view details about the movie's director, release year, and more.

Tap a Price button, and the button becomes a Rent or Buy button. Tap this button, and your purchase or rental is processed.

Figure 4-16: Shop for video in the Amazon Video Store.

Tap a Rent $ button for movies, and you see a green button labeled Rent. Tap this, and you're immediately charged for the rental. The rental period begins when you start to watch the movie.

See Chapter 8 for more about playing videos.

If you tap the Watchlist button, the item is added to your watchlist so you can go back and rent or buy it at some future time. To view your Watchlist, tap the Menu button on the Options bar when in the Videos library or store and then tap Your Watchlist. Tap any item to open a screen similar to the one shown in Figure 4-17.

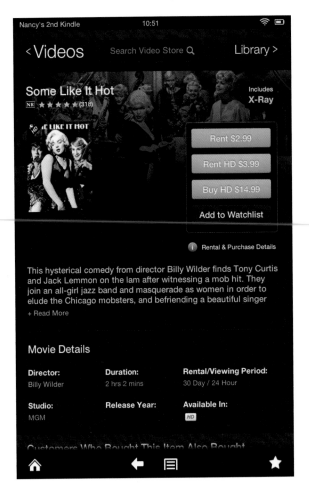

Figure 4-17: The video screen offers several options.

Shopping for Anything Else

Amazon kindly pre-installed an Amazon Shopping app on your Kindle Fire HD so that you can quickly go to their online store and buy anything your heart desires.

The Amazon Shopping app (see Figure 4-18) is included in your Apps library right out of the box. Just tap Apps from the Kindle Fire HD Home screen, and then tap the Shop Amazon app. Amazon opens in your browser with a list of recommendations for you, based on previous purchases. You can tap the Shop by Departments tab to access a drop-down list of available departments.

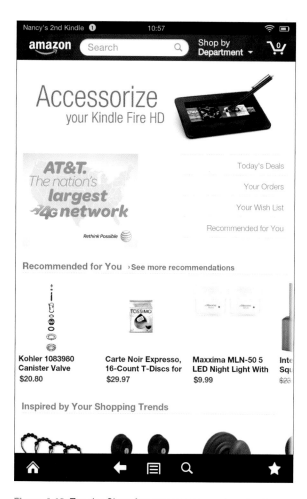

Figure 4-18: Tap the Shop Amazon app to go shopping for virtually anything.

Now, just proceed to shop as you usually do on Amazon, tapping any item of interest to add it to your cart and using your Amazon account information to pay and arrange for shipping.

5

Going Online

In This Chapter

- Using Wi-Fi on your Kindle Fire HD
- Browsing the web with Silk
- Personalizing Silk's settings
- Managing Privacy settings
- Setting up e-mail

Years ago, the best way to stay in touch with the outside world was by reading the morning paper and going to the mailbox to get your mail. Today, browsing the web and checking e-mail has replaced this routine in many of our lives. Kindle Fire HD can become your new go-to device for keeping informed and in touch by using Amazon's Silk browser and the pre-installed e-mail client.

In this chapter, you discover the ins and outs of browsing with Silk and the simple tools you can use to send and receive e-mail on Kindle Fire HD.

Getting Online by Using Wi-Fi

Except for the 8.9-inch 4G LTE version of Kindle Fire HD, Kindle Fire HD is a Wi-Fi–only device, meaning that you have to connect to a nearby Wi-Fi network to go online. You might access a Wi-Fi connection through your home network, at work, or via a public hotspot, such as an Internet cafe or airport.

When you first set up your Kindle Fire HD (as described in Chapter 2), you can choose a Wi-Fi network to use for going online. If you want to log on to a different network, follow these steps:

1. **Swipe down from the top of the Home screen to display Quick Settings which reveals a menu of common settings, such as Volume, Wireless, and Brightness.**

2. **Tap Wireless.**

   Wireless settings appear (see Figure 5-1).

3. **Tap a network in the list of available wireless networks to sign in.**

   You have to enter a password to sign in to some networks.

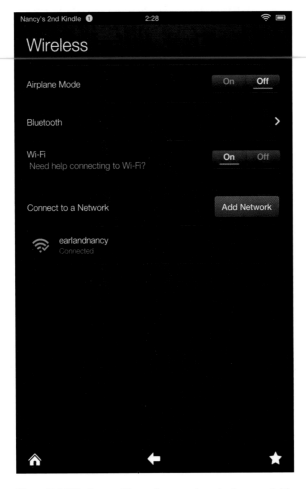

Figure 5-1: Wireless settings allow you to select an available network to join.

Browsing the Internet with Silk

Silk is a browser created by Amazon. Some people wondered why Amazon didn't choose to use an existing browser, such as Internet Explorer, for Kindle Fire HD. The answer is that Silk takes advantage of Amazon's ability to use its own servers to make your browsing experience fast.

For example, if you visit a popular news website and choose to tap the head-line story to get more details, the odds are many thousands of people have done the same thing. The Silk browser recognizes this pattern and holds that next page in its *cache* (a dedicated block of memory) to deliver it quickly to you if you also make this selection. This ability is supposed to make your browsing experience fast and smooth as, well, silk.

In the following sections, I introduce you to Silk's browser environment. Many tools and features will be familiar to you from other browsers, but a few are unique to Silk.

Using navigation tools to get around

From the Kindle Fire HD's Home screen, you can tap the Web button to display the Silk browser. You can display an Address field at any time by swiping down from just below the tab bar (don't swipe from the Status bar at the very top or you'll display the Notification screen).

Items in the Options bar help you to navigate among web pages, as shown in Figure 5-2.

You can use the Back and Forward buttons on the Options bar to move among pages you've previously viewed. To search for a page, tap the Search button, enter a site address using the onscreen keyboard, and then tap Enter. Results of the search are displayed.

Silk uses tabs that allow you to display more than one web page at a time and move among those pages. Tap the Add button in the top-right corner — which features a plus sign (+) — to add a tab in the browser. When you do, thumbnails of recently visited sites appear. You can tap on a thumbnail to go to that site, or you can tap in the Search/Address bar that appears when you add a tab and enter a URL by using the onscreen keyboard and then tap Go on the keyboard.

Home

Back

Forward

Full-Screen Mode

Menu

Search

Favorites

Figure 5-2: Silk offers a familiar browser interface.

Bookmarking sites

You can bookmark sites in Silk so that you can easily jump back to them again. You can add a Bookmark for a displayed page in a couple of ways:

✔ Swipe down just under the tabs bar to reveal the Address field and then tap the Bookmark button to the left of that field (it looks like a little ribbon with a check mark in it).

✔ With a site displayed onscreen, tap the Add button (refer to Figure 5-2) and then tap Bookmarks. Tap the Add Bookmark button in the lower-left corner of the screen.

Whichever method you use above, at this point the Add Bookmark dialog box that appears (see Figure 5-3), tap OK to bookmark the currently displayed page. You can then tap the Add button and tap Bookmarks to display thumbnails of all bookmarked pages. Tap on one to go there.

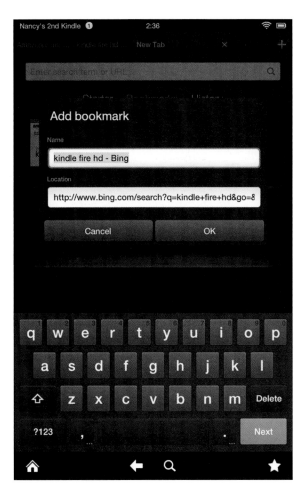

Figure 5-3: Bookmarks help you quickly return to a favorite page.

To delete a bookmark, after tapping the Bookmarks tab to display thumbnails of bookmarked pages, press and hold a page. In the menu that appears, tap Delete. In the confirming dialog box that appears, tap OK and the bookmark is removed.

When a website is open in Silk, the Menu button on the Options bar also provides a Share Page feature. When you tap this option, you can select to share the current page via e-mail.

Searching for content on a page

Web pages can contain a lot of content, so it's not always easy to find the article or discussion you want to view on a particular topic. Most browsers provide a feature to search for content on a web page, and Silk is no exception.

To search the currently displayed page by using Silk, follow these steps:

1. **Tap Menu on the Options bar.**

2. **In the list of options that appears (see Figure 5-4), tap Find in Page.**

   The onscreen keyboard appears with the Search field active.

3. **Type a search term.**

   The first instance of a match for the search term on the page appears in an orange highlight. Subsequent instances of the word on that page are highlighted in yellow, as shown in Figure 5-5.

4. **Tap any of these highlighted words to view the related content.**

5. **Tap Done to end the search.**

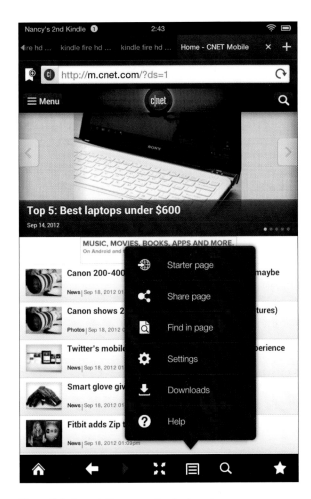

Figure 5-4: Search the currently displayed page.

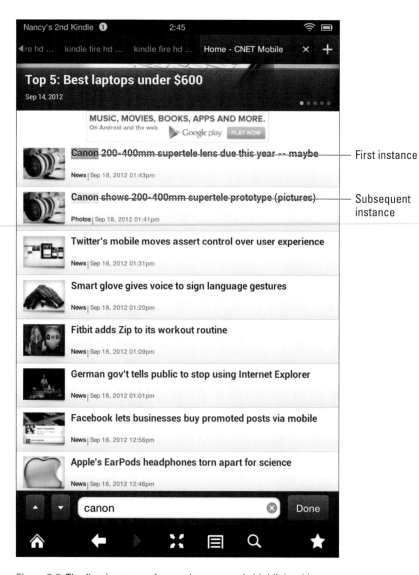

First instance

Subsequent instance

Figure 5-5: The first instance of a word on a page is highlighted in orange.

Searching the web

Most of us spend a lot of our time online browsing around to find what we want. Search engines make our lives easier because they help us narrow down what we're looking for by using specific search terms; they then troll the web to find matches for those terms from a variety of sources.

To search the entire web, follow these steps:

1. **Tap the Add button (refer to Figure 5-2) to add a tab in the browser if you want search results to appear on a new tab.**

   Thumbnails of recently visited sites appear.

2. **Tap in the Search/Address field.**

   The thumbnails change to a list of bookmarked sites, and the onscreen keyboard appears.

3. **Enter a search term in the Search/Address field and tap Go.**

   Search results appear (see Figure 5-6).

4. **Tap a result to go to that page.**

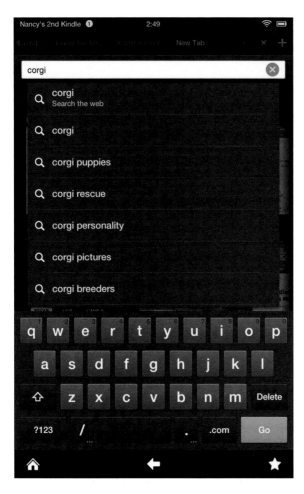

Figure 5-6: Search results are displayed in the default search engine you specify — in this case, Bing.

To specify a search engine to use other than the default, tap the Menu button in the Options bar, and then tap Settings. Tap Search Engine option to choose Bing, Google, or Yahoo! as the default search engine.

Reviewing browsing history

We've all experienced this: You know you visited a site in the last day or so that had a great deal, product, news story, or whatever — but you just can't remember the URL of the site. That's where the ability to review your browsing history comes in handy. Using this feature, you can scan the sites you visited recently organized by day and, more often than not, spot the place you want to revisit.

With Silk open, tap the Add button. Tap History, and sites you've visited on the Kindle Fire HD appear in a list divided into categories such as Today (see Figure 5-7) and Last 7 Days. Look over these sites and, when you find the one you want, tap it to go there.

To avoid losing a site you know you want to revisit, bookmark it using the procedure in the section "Bookmarking sites," earlier in this chapter.

Working with web page content

There are a few things you can do to work with contents of websites using Kindle Fire HD. For example, you may find online content, such as a PDF file, that you want to download to your Docs library or an image you want to download to the photo Gallery. You can also open or share content you find online.

Here's how these work:

- ✔ **View downloads:** Tap the Menu button on the Options bar and then tap the Downloads button to view completed downloads.

- ✔ **Save or view images:** Press and hold an image, and a menu appears offering options such as Save Image or View Image (see Figure 5-8).

- ✔ **Open, save, or share links:** Press and hold your finger on any linked text until a menu appears offering options including Open, Open in New Tab, Open in Background Tab, Bookmark Link, Share Link, and Copy Link URL.

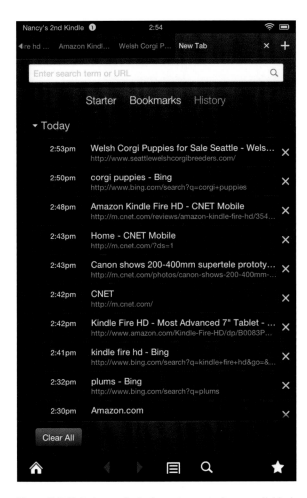

Figure 5-7: To help you find what you want, sites are divided chronologically.

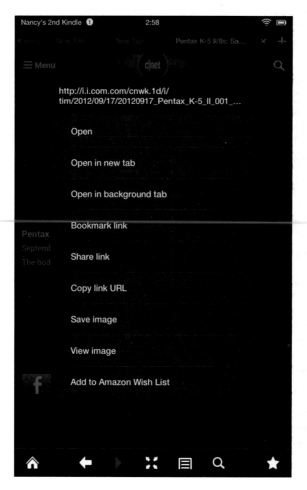

Figure 5-8: You can work with links and images on your Kindle Fire HD by using this menu.

Personalizing Silk

Silk sports a nice, clean interface. Still, there are a few things you can do to personalize the way Silk looks and acts that might work better for you.

With Silk open, tap the Menu button on the Options bar, and then tap Settings. In the screen that appears (see Figure 5-9), here are some of the things you can control about Silk behavior:

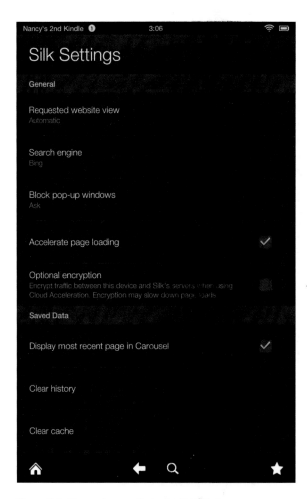

Figure 5-9: The various settings for the Silk browser.

- **Block Pop-Up Windows:** You can make settings that require Silk to ask about displaying pop-up windows, never display them, or always display them (see Figure 5-10).

- **Display Most Recent Page in Carousel:** Specify whether recently visited web pages are displayed in Kindle Fire's Carousel.

✔ **Remember Passwords:** Saves you time entering usernames and passwords for sites you visit often. Just be aware that this setting puts your accounts at risk should you ever misplace your Kindle Fire HD. One option, if you use this setting, is to require a password to unlock your Kindle Fire HD's Home screen. This setting, which can help protect all content stored on the device, is discussed in Chapter 3.

If you want to get rid of all the settings you've made to Silk, with Silk open, on the Options bar, tap the Menu button, and then tap Settings. Scroll down to Advanced Settings and then tap Reset All Settings to Default.

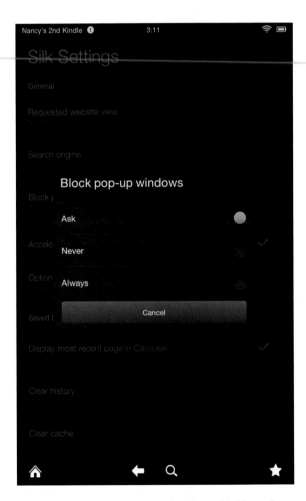

Figure 5-10: Keep those pop-up ads at bay with this setting.

Making Privacy Settings

Browsing out there on the Internet can be a bit dangerous. There are people and businesses who want to leave small files on your computer called *cookies* that they use to track your activities or gain illegal access to your online accounts.

Some uses of cookies are perfectly legitimate and allow a reputable business such as Amazon to greet you with personalized recommendations based on your past activities when you visit their sites. Less reputable sites sell your information to others or advertise based on your online history by displaying irritating pop-up windows.

The Privacy settings for Silk help you to stay safe when you're browsing online. With Silk open, tap the Menu button on the Options bar, and then tap Settings to view and modify the following privacy settings (see Figure 5-11):

- **Accept Cookies:** Tap this check box to stop sites from downloading cookies to your Kindle Fire HD.

- **Clear All Cookie Data:** You can tap this setting, and then in the Clear dialog box that appears, tap OK to clear all cookies from your device.

- **Clear Cache:** Any computing device holds information in its cache to help it redisplay a page you've visited recently, for example. To clear out that cache, which can also free up some memory on your Kindle Fire HD, tap OK.

- **Clear History:** Your Silk browser retains a history of your browsing activity to make it easy for you to revisit a site. However, it's possible for others who view your browsing history to draw conclusions about your online habits. To clear your history, tap OK in this setting.

- **Remember Form Data:** If you want Silk to remember data you've entered into forms before — such as your name, mailing address, or e-mail address — to help you complete online fields more quickly, tap this check box. The danger here, and the reason you might choose to deselect this check box, is that if somebody gets a hold of your Kindle Fire HD, they could use this feature to gain access to some of your personal information or use your online accounts.

- **Clear Form Data:** Clears out any form data you've already saved.

- **Remember Passwords.** If you want Silk to remember passwords that you enter for various accounts, tap this check box. Just be aware that this setting puts your accounts at risk should you ever misplace your Kindle Fire. One option, if you use this setting, is to require a password to unlock your Kindle Fire Home screen. This setting, which can help protect all content stored on the device, is discussed in Chapter 3.

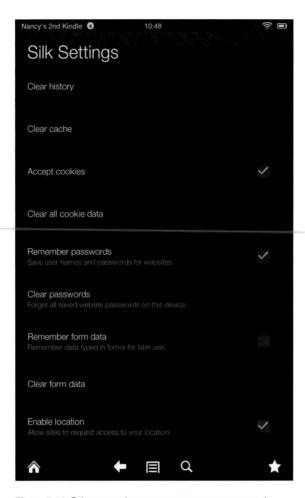

Figure 5-11: Privacy settings can protect your personal information as you browse.

✔ **Clear Passwords:** If you previously allowed Silk to remember passwords but have a change of heart, you can tap OK in this setting to remove saved passwords.

✔ **Enable Location:** Tap this check box to allow websites to request information about your physical location.

Working with E-Mail

Kindle Fire HD has a built-in e-mail client. A *client* essentially allows you to access e-mail accounts you've set up through various providers, such as Gmail and Yahoo!. You can then open the inboxes of these accounts and read, reply to, and forward messages by using your Kindle Fire HD. You can also create and send new messages, and even include attachments.

In the following sections, I provide information about setting up and using your e-mail accounts on Kindle Fire HD.

Setting up an e-mail account

Setting up your e-mail on Kindle Fire HD involves providing information about one or more e-mail accounts that you've already established with a provider such as Gmail.

Follow these steps to set up an e-mail account the first time you use the app:

1. **Swipe down from the top of the Home screen to display Settings.**

   The Quick Settings bar appears.

2. **Tap More.**

   The Settings panel appears.

3. **Tap My Account.**

4. **Tap Manage E-Mail Accounts.**

5. **Tap Add Account.**

   The dialog box shown in Figure 5-12 appears.

6. **Tap AOL, Exchange, Gmail, Hotmail, Yahoo!, or Other Provider.**

7. **Enter your username, e-mail address, and password in the appropriate fields, and then tap Next.**

   A new screen appears, displaying two fields.

8. **Enter the name that will appear on outgoing messages in the Name field and an address in the E-Mail Address field for your e-mail account.**

   The account name is optional.

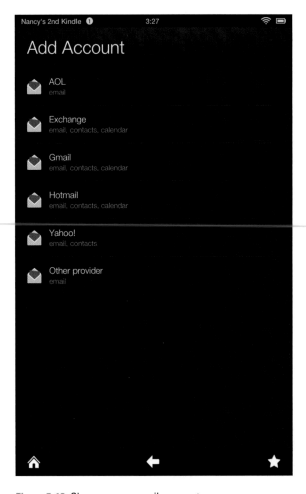

Figure 5-12: Choose your e-mail account.

9. **Enter the password for your e-mail account in the Password field.**

10. **Tap the Send Mail from This Account by Default check box if you want to set this up as your default e-mail account, and then tap Next.**

11. **If a message appears about how some accounts sync with your Kindle Fire HD, tap OK to proceed.**

12. **In the final screen, tap Save and then tap the View Inbox button (see Figure 5-13) to go to the inbox for the account you just set up.**

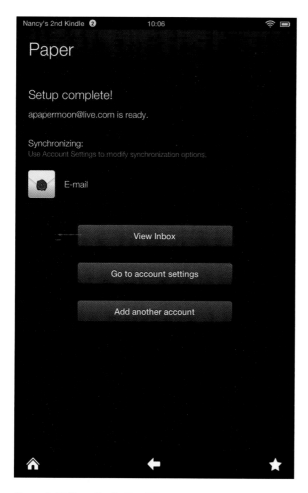

Figure 5-13: Your Kindle Fire HD e-mail setup is complete.

You can set up as many e-mail accounts as you like. When you open the Kindle Fire HD Email app, you see a Unified Inbox that combines messages from all accounts you set up, as well as individual inboxes for each account.

Sending e-mail

After you set up your e-mail account(s), as described in the preceding section, you're able to send e-mails from your Kindle Fire HD. To create and send an e-mail, with the Email app and an e-mail account inbox open, follow these steps:

1. **Tap the New button.**

   A blank e-mail form appears, as shown in Figure 5-14.

2. **In the To field, enter a name.**

   Alternatively, tap the Add Contact button (refer to Figure 5-14) to open the Contacts app and tap on a name there to add that person as an addressee.

Figure 5-14: A blank form waiting for you to enter an e-mail address, subject, and message.

3. **If you want to send a copy of the e-mail to somebody, tap the Options button (refer to Figure 5-14) to make those fields appear; then enter addresses or choose them from the Contacts app by tapping the Add Contact button.**

4. **Tap in the Subject field and enter a subject by using the onscreen keyboard.**

5. **Tap in the Message text field and enter a message.**

6. **(Optional) If you want to add an attachment to an e-mail, tap the Attach button to the right of the Cc field and, in the menu that appears, choose to attach an item from the Photos app, OfficeSuite, or Personal Videos.**

7. **To send your message, tap the Send button (refer to Figure 5-14).**

   If you decide you're not ready to send the message quite yet, you also have the option of tapping the Cancel button and then tapping Save Draft.

Here are a couple of handy shortcuts for entering text in your e-mail: The Auto Complete feature lists possible word matches as you type; tap one to complete a word. In addition, you can double-tap the spacebar to place a period and space at the end of a sentence.

Receiving e-mail

Kindle Fire HD can receive your e-mail messages whenever you're connected to a Wi-Fi network.

When an e-mail is delivered to your inbox (see Figure 5-15), simply tap to open it. Read it and contemplate whether you want to save it or delete it (or forward or reply to it, as covered in the following section). If you don't need to keep the message, you can delete it by tapping the Delete button at the top of the screen.

If you're expecting an e-mail but don't see it in your inbox, try tapping the Menu button in the top-right corner of the screen and then tapping on Refresh. This pulls any new e-mails into your inbox.

Forwarding and replying to e-mail

When you receive an e-mail, you can choose to reply to the sender, reply to the sender and anybody else who was included as an addressee on the original message, or forward the e-mail to another person.

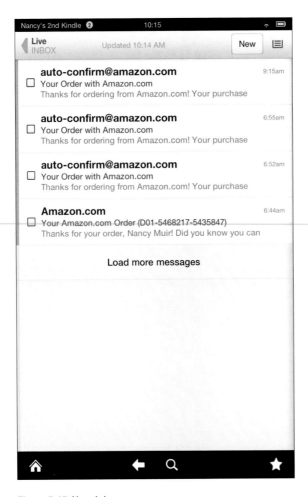

Figure 5-15: Your inbox.

 If you reply to all recipients, you send an answer to the sender, anybody else in the To field of the original message, and anybody in the Cc and Bcc fields. Because Bcc fields aren't visible to you as a recipient, you may be sending your reply to people you're not aware of.

To forward or reply to an e-mail, with the Email app inbox displayed, follow these steps:

1. **Tap an e-mail to open it.**

2. **Tap the Respond button.**

   A menu of options appears.

3. **Tap Reply, Reply All, or Forward (see Figure 5-16).**

4. **If you're forwarding the message, enter a new recipient.**

   If you're replying, the message is already addressed, but you can enter additional recipients if you want to.

5. **Tap in the message area and enter your message.**

6. **Tap the Send button to send your message on its way.**

Figure 5-16: Choose to reply to a message or send it on to somebody else.

When you read a message, you can tell that it has been marked as read when the sender's name is no longer shown in bold. To mark it as unread again, perhaps to draw your attention to it so you read it again, tap on the box to the left of the e-mail in your inbox and then tap the Mark button in the top-right corner of the screen. To delete an e-mail from your inbox, select it and tap the Delete button.

Sending E-Mail to Your Kindle Account

When you register your Kindle Fire HD, you get an associated e-mail account, which essentially allows you or others to e-mail documents in Word, PDF, RTF, or HTML format to your Kindle Fire HD.

The address of the account is displayed in the Docs library. Tap the Docs Library button on the Home screen, and then tap the Cloud button; you see a line that reads Send Documents to `YourE-MailAccount@kindle.com` where `Your E-Mail Account` is the name of your Kindle e-mail account.

You or others can e-mail documents to this address, and those documents automatically appear in your Docs library. Note that you might need to go to Amazon by using a browser and change the approved e-mail accounts. Click on Your Account and then on Manage Your Kindle in the Digital Content section. Click the Personal Document Settings link on the left side of the screen and make sure the account is listed under Send to Kindle Email Settings as Approved.

Part III
Having Fun and Getting Productive

The 5th Wave   By Rich Tennant

"What I'm doing should clear your sinuses, take away your headache, and charge your Kindle Fire HD."

In this part . . .

In this part, you can begin to explore the wealth of multimedia and written content Kindle Fire HD makes available to you. You get to know the Kindle e-reader and how to subscribe to and read periodicals; you also find out how all this content is coordinated among your devices using Amazon's Whispersync technology. Chapters 7 and 8 are where you read about playing music and videos on your Kindle Fire HD. Chapter 9 gets you connected to others as you manage contacts, and make calls over the Internet using Kindle Fire HD and the Skype app, while Chapter 10 talks about getting productive by working with documents.

6

E-Reader Extraordinaire

Kindle Fire HD comes from a family of e-readers, so it's only natural that the e-reader you use to read books and magazines on the device is a very robust feature. With its bright, colorful screen, Kindle Fire HD broadens your reading experience beyond black and white books to color publications such as magazines or graphic novels. Its easy-to-use controls help you navigate publications, bookmark and highlight text, and search your libraries of print content.

In this chapter, you can discover what's available, how you open publications, and how to read and then delete them from Kindle Fire HD when you're done. You also explore the possibilities of Amazon's lending library and how to lend books to your friends and borrow books from your local public library.

So Many Things to Read!

Amazon started as an online book retailer, although through the years, it has branched out to become the largest retailer of just about everything on the planet. Kindle Fire HD makes it easy for you to buy your content from Amazon. Although you can buy and sideload content from other sources to Kindle Fire HD, buying from Amazon ensures that you're dealing with a reputable company and receiving safe content (uncontaminated by malware).

The content you buy from Amazon is automatically downloaded to your Kindle device, which means that not only is buying from Amazon's bookstore easy, but you can take advantage of their vast selection of books. In addition, you can borrow Kindle versions of books from the Amazon Lending Library, as well as borrowing from many public libraries. You can also lend books to your friends.

Amazon has also made deals to make many of your favorite magazines and newspapers available. With magazines and newspapers, you can buy the current issue or subscribe to get multiple issues sent to your Kindle Fire HD as they become available.

Buying books

To buy books or magazines for your Kindle Fire HD, on the Home screen, tap either the Books or Newsstand button, which takes you to your Books or Magazine library.

Tap the Store button; this takes you to the Amazon Kindle bookstore, shown in Figure 6-1. See Chapter 4 for more about how to search for and buy content.

You can also buy content at the Amazon website from your computer and have it download to your Kindle Fire HD. Just select what device you want it delivered to from the drop-down list below the Add to Cart button before you buy Kindle content.

Amazon uses a technology called Whispersync to download books and magazines to your devices. All but the 8.9-inch 4G LTE model of Kindle Fire HD require a Wi-Fi connection, so you need to be connected to a Wi-Fi hotspot to download publications.

Using the Amazon Lending Library

On the screen that appears when you enter the Store (see the preceding section), you'll see a Kindle Owners' Lending Library link on the right side of the page. Tap this link and a list of free lending selections appears (see Figure 6-2).

These free items are only available if you have an Amazon Prime membership.

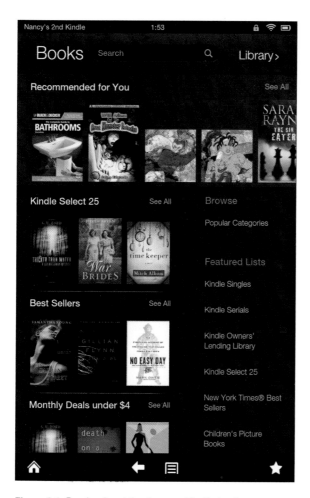

Figure 6-1: Buy books at the Amazon Kindle bookstore.

Tap on an item and a descriptive page appears. Tap the Borrow for Free button and your selection is immediately downloaded. You can borrow a title from the Lending Library approximately every two weeks.

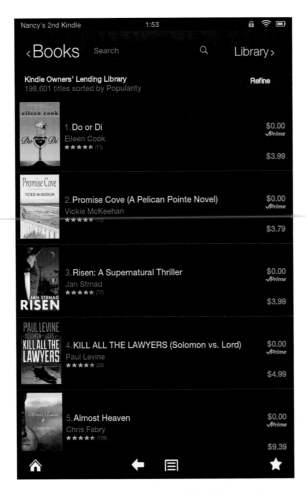

Figure 6-2: These selections are free if you have an Amazon Prime account.

Borrowing from your local library

More than 11,000 libraries in the United States lend Kindle versions of books through a system called Overdrive, which allows you to easily download books to your Kindle Fire HD. The time you can borrow a book varies by library, and each library may have a slightly different system for borrowing books.

Here are the typical steps for borrowing Kindle books from your library, but you should ask your library for the specific steps that work with their system:

1. Go to your library's website and search for e-books.

   Note that you'll need a library card and PIN to borrow books.

2. Click the title you want to check out and then enter your library card information and PIN.

3. After you check out a title, choose the Get for Kindle option.

   You may then have to enter your Amazon.com account information to borrow the title.

4. Choose the title and the device you want the book delivered to; then choose Get Library Book to download the title to your Kindle Fire HD.

Reading Books

After you own some Kindle books, you can begin to read by using the simple e-reader tools in the Kindle e-reader app. You may have used this app on another device, such as your computer, smartphone, or tablet, though each version of this app has slightly different features. In the following sections, I go over the basics of how the Kindle e-reader app works on Kindle Fire HD.

You can get to the Home screen from anywhere in the e-reader app. If a Home button isn't visible, just tap the page to display the Options bar, which includes a Home button and a set of tools for navigating a book.

Going to the (Books) library

When you tap Books on your Kindle Fire HD screen, you open the Books library, containing downloaded content on the Device tab and content in the Cloud on the Cloud tab (see Figure 6-3). The active tab is the one displaying orange text. There's also a Store button you use to go to Amazon's website and shop for books.

There are also several features in your Books library that you can use to get different perspectives on its contents:

 ✏ **Grid and List views:** Tap the Menu button on the Options bar to display the Grid View and List View options. These provide views of your books by using large thumbnails on a bookshelf (Grid view, shown in Figure 6-4) or in a text list including title and author, along with an accompanying small thumbnail.

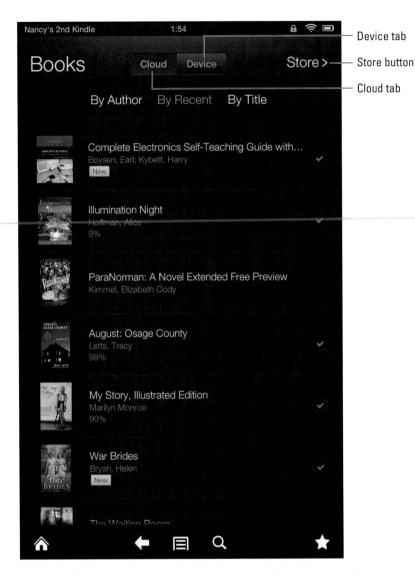

Figure 6-3: The Books library displays all your book purchases on two tabs.

✓ **Sort titles:** Use the By Author, By Recent, and By Title buttons near the top of the screen to view books by any of these three criteria.

✓ **Identify new titles:** If you've just downloaded but haven't started reading a book, there will be a banner in the corner of the thumbnail with the word New on it (see Figure 6-5).

Figure 6-4: The Grid view in the Books library.

Tap the Search button on the Options bar to search your Books library contents by title or author.

Opening a book

Ah, the pleasure you had as a child in opening up a new book, awaiting the adventures or knowledge it had to impart! Opening your first e-book is likely to bring you a similar sort of pleasure.

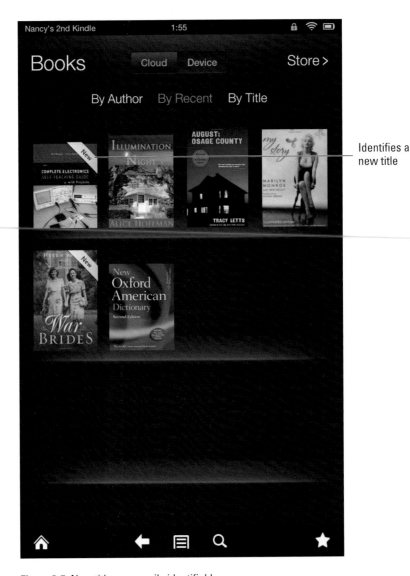

Identifies a new title

Figure 6-5: New titles are easily identifiable.

To open a book from the Home screen, tap Books to open the Books library. Locate the book you want to read (swipe upward if you need to reveal more books in the list) and simply tap it. If the book has not been downloaded to your Kindle Fire HD, it begins to download and takes only seconds to complete.

If you never started to read the book, it opens on its title page. If you've read part of the book, it opens automatically to the last page you read. This last read page is bookmarked in the Cloud by Amazon when you stop reading, so no matter what device you use to read it — your Kindle Fire HD, computer, or smartphone, for example — you go to the last read page immediately.

You can also open a publication from Favorites or the Carousel. Read more about these features in Chapter 2.

Navigating a book

An open book just begs to be read. You're used to flipping pages in a physical book, but an e-reader provides you with several ways to move around it.

The simplest way to move one page forward or one page back is to tap your finger anywhere on the right or left side of the page, respectively. Try this to move from the title page to a page of text within the book. With a book page displayed, tap it to see these buttons along the bottom of the screen (see Figure 6-6):

- **Home:** Located in the bottom-left corner, this button takes you to the Kindle Fire HD Home screen.

- **Back:** Tap the button of a left-pointing arrow to go back one screen (not page).

- **Search:** Use the magnifying glass button found in the middle of the screen to initiate a search for text in the book.

- **Favorites:** Tap this button to see a list of Favorites, which includes items from just about any category of content or apps that you want to access quickly.

In addition to the tools at the bottom of the screen, you find these options along the top of the screen:

- **Settings:** Tap this button to make adjustments to the fonts and font size, page color, and margins, or to enable Text-to-Speech to have Kindle Fire HD read the book to you.

- **Go To:** Use this button to access additional locations including going to a specific page or location; syncing to the furthest read page; or viewing the beginning, cover, or front matter, or any chapter in the book.

- **Notes:** Displays any notes you have made in the book.

✔ **X–Ray:** Tap this button to view additional information about the book if it's available for that title.

✔ **Share:** Use this button to share your thoughts about the book via Twitter or Facebook.

✔ **Bookmark:** Places a bookmark on the page.

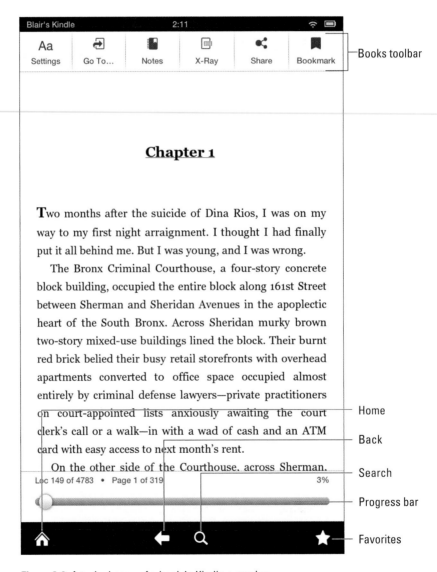

Figure 6-6: A typical page of a book in Kindle e-reader.

Reading children's books

Many children's books with extensive illustrations use what Amazon refers to as a *fixed layout,* meaning that the pages are fixed representations of how the pages look in the print book. This means that you can't enlarge and reduce the size of everything on the page at one time, you can't change the font style, and you can't change orientation: Each book is set in either landscape or portrait orientation. To move from page to page, you can swipe from right to left on the right page to flip it over.

Keep in mind that children's books are usually set up with blocks of text that go along with illustrations; that's why you can't enlarge text on an entire page; instead, you enlarge a single block of text. To do this, double-tap a block of text, and the text becomes larger. When you subsequently swipe the page, you move to the next block of text, which enlarges (the previous block of text goes back to normal size). When you've read the last block of text on the page (typically in a two-page spread), swiping takes you to the next page. Double-tap the currently enlarged text again to go back to normal text size and proceed through the book.

Although the Option bar choices and Progress bar are the same as in other books, pressing the Settings button in a children's book results in the message Font Style Options Are Not Available for This Title.

The Progress bar along the bottom of the screen (refer to Figure 6-6) indicates how far along in the publication you are at the moment. To move around the publication, you can press the circle on this bar and drag it in either direction.

Searching in a book

Want to find that earlier reference to a character so that you can keep up with a plot? Or do you want to find any mention of Einstein in an e-encyclopedia? To find words or phrases in a book, you can use the Search feature.

Follow these steps to search a book:

1. **With a book open, tap the page to display the Options bar, if necessary.**

2. **Tap the Search button at the bottom of the page.**

   The Search field and onscreen keyboard are displayed, as shown in Figure 6-7.

3. **Enter a search term or phrase and then tap the Go key on the keyboard.**

   Search results are displayed, as shown in Figure 6-8.

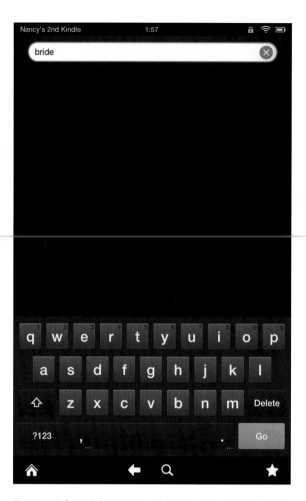

Figure 6-7: Search for a word or phrase by using the Search field and onscreen keyboard.

If you'd rather search the web, press a word or phrase to highlight it, and then in the resulting dialog box, tap the More button. At this point, you can tap either Search in Book, Search Wikipedia, or Search the Web. The Search the Web option takes you to search results for the term in the Bing search engine, and the Wikipedia option takes you to the entry in the popular online encyclopedia that matches your search term. Tap the Back button when you want to return to the e-reader app.

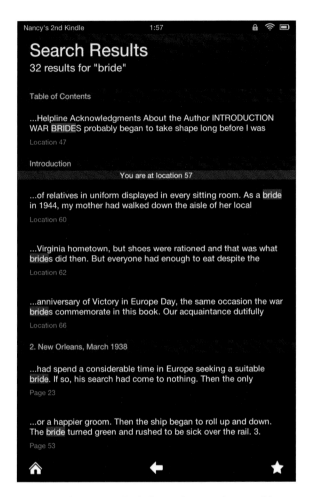

Figure 6-8: Search results indicate the search term with a highlight.

Bookmarking a page and highlighting text

If you find that perfect quote or a word you just have to read again at a later time, you can use the Bookmark feature in Kindle e-reader.

To place a bookmark on a page, display the page and tap it to reveal the Bookmark button (the tool in the top-right corner of the page), and then tap the Bookmark button. A small bookmark ribbon appears on the page (see Figure 6-9).

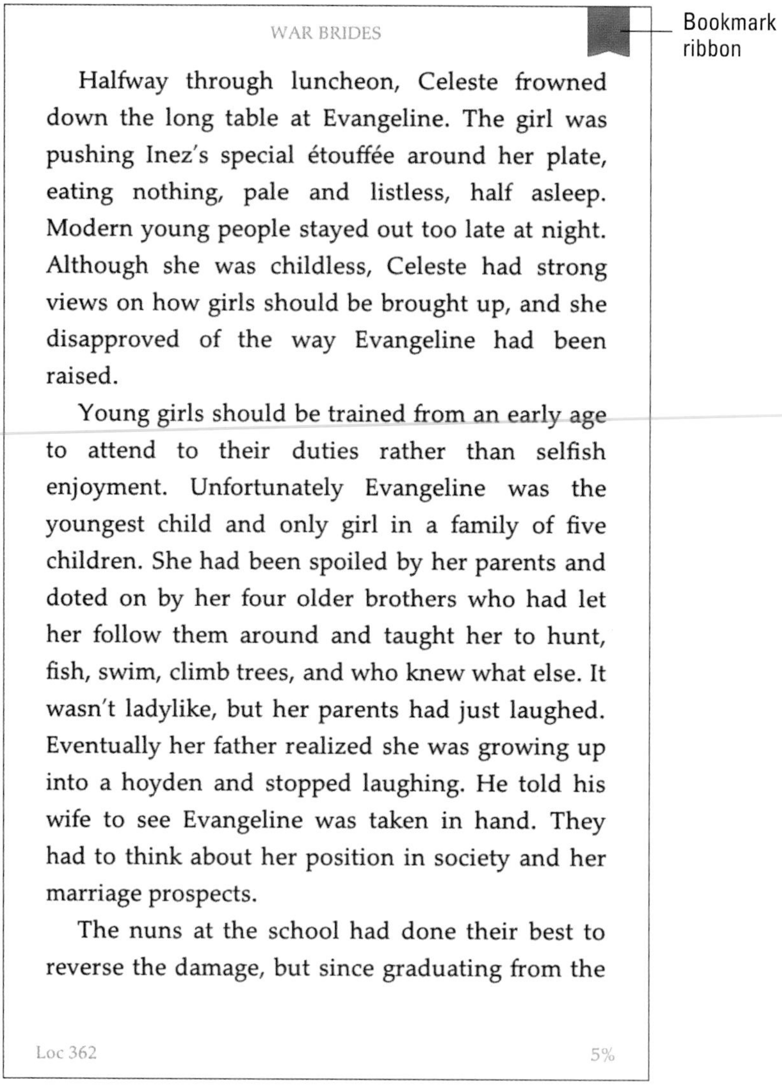

WAR BRIDES

Halfway through luncheon, Celeste frowned down the long table at Evangeline. The girl was pushing Inez's special étouffée around her plate, eating nothing, pale and listless, half asleep. Modern young people stayed out too late at night. Although she was childless, Celeste had strong views on how girls should be brought up, and she disapproved of the way Evangeline had been raised.

Young girls should be trained from an early age to attend to their duties rather than selfish enjoyment. Unfortunately Evangeline was the youngest child and only girl in a family of five children. She had been spoiled by her parents and doted on by her four older brothers who had let her follow them around and taught her to hunt, fish, swim, climb trees, and who knew what else. It wasn't ladylike, but her parents had just laughed. Eventually her father realized she was growing up into a hoyden and stopped laughing. He told his wife to see Evangeline was taken in hand. They had to think about her position in society and her marriage prospects.

The nuns at the school had done their best to reverse the damage, but since graduating from the

Loc 362   5%

Bookmark ribbon

Figure 6-9: A bookmarked page.

To highlight text, press and hold your finger on the text. Small handles appear on either side, as shown in Figure 6-10. If you want to select additional adjacent text to be highlighted, press your finger on one of these triangular handles and drag to the left or right. When the entire phrase or paragraph you want to highlight is selected, tap Highlight.

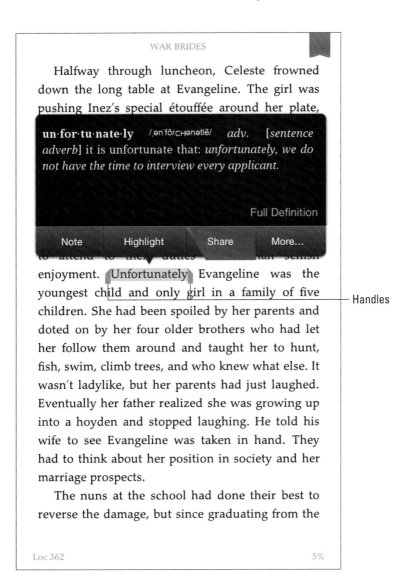

Figure 6-10: Tap either handle to enlarge the area of selected text.

When you place a bookmark on a page or highlight text within a book, you can then display a list of bookmarks and highlights by tapping the page and then tapping the Notes button at the top of the page to display your notes and marks (see Figure 6-11). You can jump to the page indicated by a bookmark or to highlighted text by tapping an item in this list.

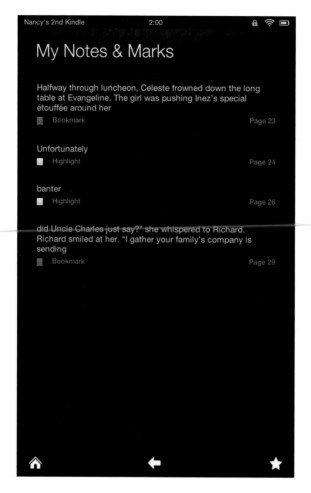

Figure 6-11: Both highlights and bookmarks are listed.

When you press text and see the menu shown in Figure 6-11, a brief definition appears from the pre-installed *New Oxford American Dictionary*. In the definition window, tap Full Definition to go to the full Oxford dictionary definition. Tap the Back button to return to the book. See Chapter 10 for more about Kindle Fire HD's built-in dictionary.

Modifying the appearance of a page

There are several things you can do to control how things appear on a page in Kindle e-reader. First, you can make text larger or smaller and change the font. Second, you can choose a white, black, or sepia-toned background for a page. Finally, you can adjust the width of margins.

To control all these settings, tap the page to display the Options bar, and then tap the Settings button (the one with a capital and lowercase A) in the top-left corner of the screen. The options shown in Figure 6-12 appear:

- **Font Size:** Tap a particular font sample to change the size.

- **Color Mode:** Tap a setting to display a different color page background. A white background will give you black text on a white page. A black background gives you white text on a black page. A sepia background gives you a pale tan background and black text which may make reading easier on your eyes, for example.

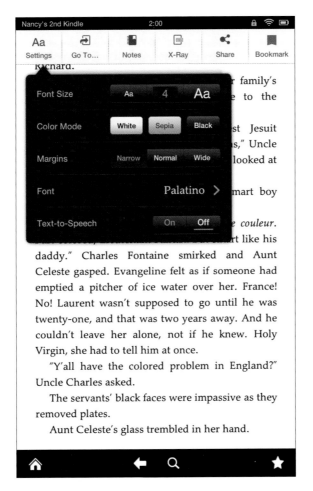

Figure 6-12: Settings options offer you some control over the appearance of your pages.

✏ **Margins:** Choose the margin setting you prefer.

✏ **Font:** Select a different font for the page.

The Text-to-Speech setting in the Kindle e-reader settings allows you turn on a feature that reads text to you in English for titles that have this feature enabled. You can choose from three reading speeds, but the only voice available is a female voice. With an enabled e-book displayed, tap to display the progress bar and tools along the top, and then tap the Play button to the left of the progress bar. The audio begins. Tap the Play button again to stop the text to speech feature.

You can adjust brightness manually or have Kindle Fire HD do it automatically. Go to the Home screen and swipe down from the top of the screen to reveal the Quick Settings bar, and then tap the Brightness button. If you turn Automatic Brightness on, the Kindle Fire HD will adjust brightness of the screen to compensate for ambient light conditions. If you turn Automatic Brightness off, you can press the circle on the slider and move it to the left or right to adjust brightness.

Sharing with others

When you're reading a book, you can share your thoughts with others via Facebook or Twitter and let them know how you liked the book. Follow these steps to share your thoughts on a book:

1. **With a book open, tap the screen to display the tools shown in Figure 6-13.**

2. **Tap the Share button near the top-right corner of the screen.**

3. **In the screen that appears (see Figure 6-14), tap in the text field at the top of the page and then use the onscreen keyboard to enter a message.**

4. **Tap the Share button to share your thoughts on the book with others. If you want to share via Twitter or Facebook use the buttons beneath the Shared Notes & Highlights text field.**

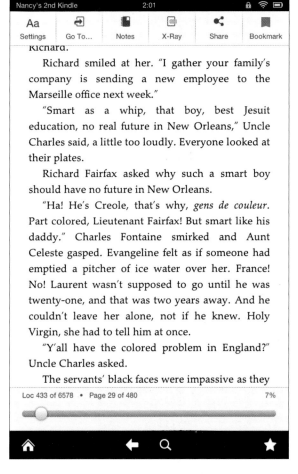

Figure 6-13: e-reader tools help you read and share your thoughts.

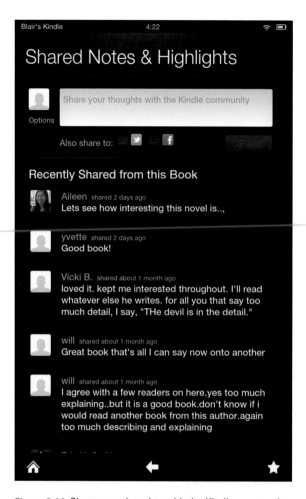

Figure 6-14: Share your thoughts with the Kindle community.

Managing Publications

After you purchase content on Amazon, from apps to music and books, that content is archived in your Amazon Cloud library. If you finish reading a book on Kindle Fire HD, you can remove it from your device. The book is still in the Amazon Cloud, and you can re-download it to your Kindle Fire HD at any time when you're connected to a Wi-Fi network.

To remove a book or magazine from your Kindle Fire HD libraries, follow these steps:

1. **On the Home screen, tap Books or Newsstand to display your library.**
2. **Locate and press your finger on the item you want to remove.**

   A menu appears (see Figure 6-15).
3. **Tap Remove from Device.**

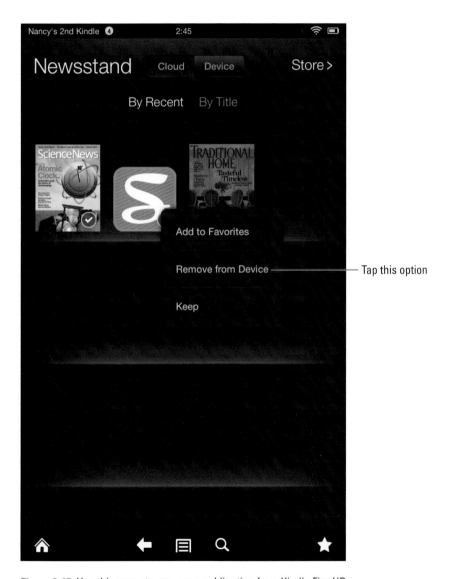

Figure 6-15: Use this menu to remove a publication from Kindle Fire HD.

The thumbnail of the item remains in your Books library on the Cloud tab and on the Carousel or Favorites if you've placed it there. To download and read the book again, just double-tap it in any of these locations, and the download begins.

Unlike video and music, which you can stream from the Cloud without ever downloading them, books, magazines, and newspapers can't be read from the Cloud; they must be downloaded to a Kindle device before you can read them.

If you download a periodical and then press your finger on it in Newsstand, you see the Keep or Remove from Device options shown in Figure 6-15. At some point, old issues will be removed from your device unless you choose to keep them by using the Keep command.

Book samples will offer only a Delete option when you get to Step 3 above. The *New Oxford American Dictionary* offers only the option of adding it to Favorites because it's pre-installed by Amazon.

Buying and Reading Periodicals

Reading magazines and newspapers on your Kindle Fire HD is similar to reading books, with a few important differences. You navigate magazines a bit differently and can display them in two different views.

Follow these steps to buy and read a magazine or newspaper:

1. **From the Home screen, tap Newsstand.**

2. **Tap Store.**

3. **Tap a periodical and then tap Subscribe Now or Buy Issue to buy it.**

4. **Return to Newsstand and tap a magazine or newspaper in the Newsstand to read it.**

   Alternatively, you can tap an item on the Carousel from the Home screen.

   If the publication hasn't been downloaded to the device, it begins to download now.

5. **Tap near the edge of the screen and thumbnails of all pages in the publication are displayed along the bottom of the screen just above the Options bar (see Figure 6-16).**

6. **Swipe right or left to scroll through these pages or drag the scroll bar indicator left or right.**

Figure 6-16: Scroll through thumbnails of pages to find the one you want.

7. When you find the page you want, tap that page to display it full-screen.

The Menu button on the Options bar displays contents of the current issue.

8. Tap an item in the table of contents to go to that item.

As with books, in most publications, you can double-tap to enlarge text on the page; double-tap again to reduce the size of the text. You can also pinch and unpinch the touchscreen to move between larger and smaller views of a page's contents.

Some periodicals can appear in two views:

✔ **Text view:** In Text view, you see articles in more of an e-reader format (meaning that you get larger text with no columns and no images). If a publication supports Text view, double-tapping the screen will present the contents in that view. In Text view, there's a Font button on the Options bar offering Font Style and Typeface tabs to adjust the size and font used for text. There's also a Style choice for changing Size, Margins, and Color Mode (page background).

Double-tap to return from Text view to Page view.

✔ **Page view:** Page view shows an exact image of the publication's pages, with all columns and photos intact. You can scroll through the magazine, view it in landscape or portrait orientation, and pinch and unpinch to zoom in and out of the pages.

In Page view, you can tap the Font tool on the Options bar to turn the page curl effect off. This effect seems to roll the current page as you flick with your finger to flip to the next page.

Reading docs on Kindle Fire HD

Reading docs on your Kindle Fire HD is a much more straightforward proposition than reading e-books (meaning there are fewer things you can do to navigate around a doc or format the appearance of text). Tap the Docs button on the Home screen, and then locate and tap a document; or tap a doc on the Carousel or Favorites to open it.

Swipe left or right to move from page to page or use the slider that appears along the bottom of the screen when the Options bar is displayed to move around the document.

In OfficeSuite docs, you can make notes and highlights, but not in PDF documents. To do this in an OfficeSuite doc, press a word to display a menu, and then tap Note or Highlight in that menu. You can read more about docs and Kindle Fire HD in Chapter 10.

7

Playing Music

Music has become ubiquitous in most of our lives. Portable devices provide us with decent-quality sound systems for listening to everything from Lady Gaga to Mozart, everywhere from the subway to the jogging path.

The ability to tap into Amazon's tremendous Music Store (with over 20 million songs at the time of this writing) and *sideload* (transfer) music from other sources by using the Kindle Fire HD's Micro USB cable means that you can build up your ideal music library and take it with you wherever you go.

Also, the addition of Dolby Digital Plus audio powered through dual-driver stereo speakers provides one of the finest listening experiences in the world of tablets. This system even optimizes sound for what you're playing so music sounds like music rather than movie dialog, and music through Kindle Fire HD's speakers plays one way while music through headsets is optimized for that environment.

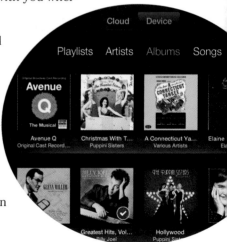

In this chapter, you learn about getting music onto your Kindle Fire HD (see Chapter 4 for more about shopping for music) and how to use the simple tools in the library to play your music and create playlists.

Exploring the Music Library

All your music is stored in the Music library (see Figure 7-1), which you display by tapping the Music button on the Kindle Fire HD Home screen. The currently playing or last played song and playback controls are located at the bottom of the screen.

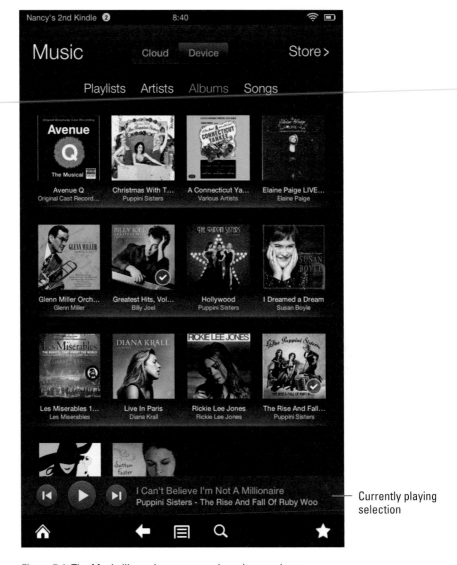

Currently playing selection

Figure 7-1: The Music library is your central music repository.

The library is organized by Playlists, Artists, as shown in Figure 7-2, Albums, and Songs. Tap on any of these tabs to display the associated content.

At the bottom of the screen, in the Options bar, is a Back arrow to move you back one screen in the library, the Menu button, and a Search icon to help you find pieces of music.

Figure 7-2: The Artists tab shows available content by performer.

Music library settings

If you swipe down from the top of Kindle Fire HD's screen and tap More in Quick Settings, you can then tap Applications, scroll down, and tap Music. When you do, you see two settings:

✓ **Clear Cache:** This clears any data that has been stored to speed up future music downloads.

✓ **Automatic Downloads:** This setting allows you to choose to automatically download selections to your Kindle Fire HD whenever you save them to the Amazon Cloud.

If you tap the Menu button, you see four additional options:

✓ **List View:** This option displays your music with smaller icons in a list (see Figure 7-3) rather than a grid, with an arrow next to each item in the list that you can tap to display more details. You can also just tap on the thumbnail of the artist, song, or album to proceed to details and play the selection.

✓ **Downloads:** Tap Downloads to see items in the process of downloading, as well as completed downloads.

✓ **Clear Queue:** This setting will appear in the menu only when you're displaying the currently playing music. From the list of songs in an album, tap Now Playing to display the currently playing music full screen with music playback controls. If you are displaying the full screen of the currently playing music, tap the Clear Queue command to stop the music and go back to the Music library home screen.

✓ **Help:** Tap Help to get more information about using the Music app.

When you tap the Search button on the Options bar, you bring up the Search field. Tap in the field and enter the title of a piece of music or a performer, and then tap Go on the onscreen keyboard. Kindle Fire HD displays results on each of the tabs in the Music library that match the search term(s).

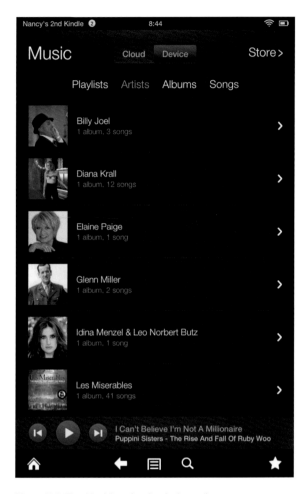

Figure 7-3: The List View for the Artists tab.

Uploading Music to the Cloud

One way to add music to your Kindle Fire HD Music library is by buying it from the Amazon Music Store.

You can also transfer a musical selection or collection stored on your computer (the music you've bought through iTunes, for example) by using the Kindle Fire HD's Micro USB cable. (Read more about this process in Chapter 2.)

In addition, the Amazon Cloud allows you to upload music from your computer; after you upload music, it's available to you through your Kindle Fire HD Music library.

Any MP3s you've purchased online from Amazon are automatically stored in the Amazon Cloud. For items you've imported, the first 250 are stored for free.

Follow these steps to upload music to the Amazon Cloud:

1. **Go to** `www.amazon.com/cloudplayer` **on your PC or Mac.**

2. **Sign into your Amazon account.**

   The page shown in Figure 7-4 is displayed.

Figure 7-4: The Amazon Cloud Player is where all your Amazon-purchased music resides.

3. **Click the Import Your Music button.**

   A dialog box appears, asking you to get the Amazon Music Importer.

4. **Click Download Now and follow the instructions that appear to install the Amazon Music Importer.**

5. **After the Amazon Music Importer has been installed, click to authorize your device.**

   You see the Amazon Cloud Player dialog box shown in Figure 7-5.

6. **Click the Start Scan button.**

   If you'd rather pick the items to import yourself, click the Browse Manually button. The following screen lists the number of songs that were found.

7. **Click the Import Now button.**

   A dialog box appears showing your import progress. You can click the Pause Import button at any time if you want to stop the import process.

After you upload items to your Amazon Cloud library, they're available to Kindle Fire HD on the Cloud tab of the Music library (see Figure 7-6).

Figure 7-5: Tap into all your music by using the Amazon Music Importer.

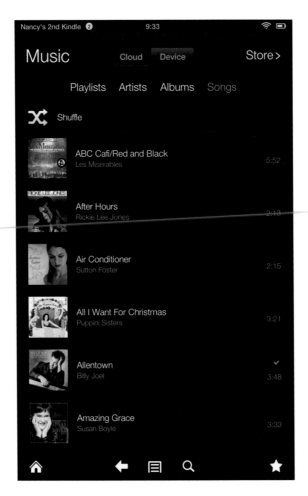

Figure 7-6: Music stored in the Amazon Cloud Player listed in your Kindle Fire HD library.

Playing Music

After you have some music available to play (which I explain how to do in the preceding sections), playing that music is an easy task, one that will make fine use of your experience with every other music player you've ever encountered.

Kindle Fire HD's dual speakers are on the back of the device, so for the best listening experience, turn your device around and definitely remove any surrounding cover or case from the back side!

Opening and playing a song

First, you have to locate an item to play, and then you can use the playback toolbar to control the playback. Follow these steps to play music from your Music library:

1. **Tap the Music button on the Kindle Fire HD's Home screen.**

2. **Locate an item you want to play on a tab in the Music library, such as Songs or Artists.**

3. **If you open a tab other than Songs, you need to tap to open an album or playlist to view the contents.**

4. **Tap to play the song.**

   If you tap the first song in a group of music selections, such as an album or playlist, Kindle Fire HD begins to play all selections, starting with the one you tapped.

5. **Use the controls shown in Figure 7-7 to control playback.**

Tap the back-facing arrow on the Options bar or the Hide button in the top-left corner of a currently playing song to go back to the album or playlist the song belongs to. To go back to the Now Playing screen for the song, tap the information bar for the song that appears along the bottom of the screen (see Figure 7-8).

You can adjust playback volume by swiping down from the top of the Kindle Fire HD screen to reveal Quick Settings and then tapping Volume, or use the Volume setting in the Now Playing controls.

Creating playlists

Playlists allow you to create collections of songs that transcend the boundaries of albums or artists. For example, you might want to create a playlist for a romantic evening, a dance party, or a mellow road trip.

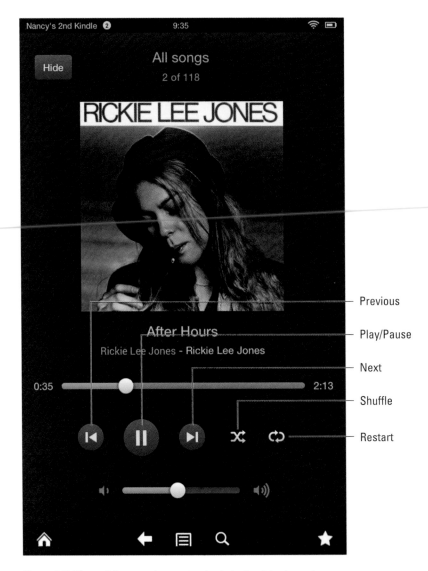

Figure 7-7: Most of these tools are standard playback tools you've probably seen before.

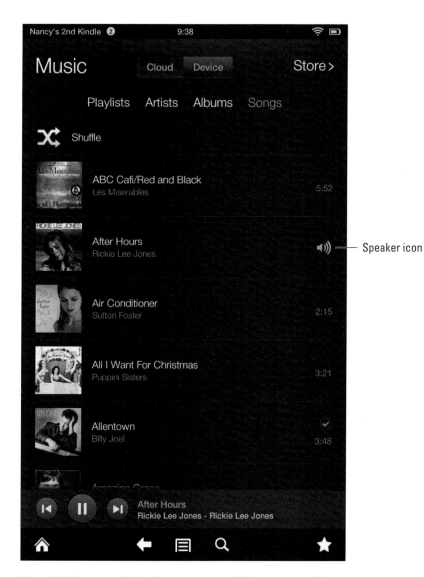

Speaker icon

Figure 7-8: The currently playing song sports a little orange speaker in this list.

Getting sound out by cord or Bluetooth

If you want to use a set of headphones with your Kindle Fire HD, which can improve the sound and remove extraneous noise, plug a compatible headphone into the headphone jack on the top of the device, near the Power button.

Alternately, you can use the Kindle Fire HD's Bluetooth capability to connect to a Bluetooth headset or speakers. To enable Bluetooth, swipe down from the top of the screen to view Quick Settings, tap Wireless, and then tap Bluetooth. Tap the Enable Bluetooth On button. Kindle Fire HD searches for nearby Bluetooth devices, but if it doesn't find yours, you can manually initiate a scan by tapping the Search for Devices button.

When you tap Music on the Home screen, you see the Playlists tab. Tap it, and you see a Create New Playlist button and two default playlists, Purchases and Recently Added to Cloud (see Figure 7-9). If you have created other playlists, they appear on this screen, as well.

To create a new playlist, follow these steps:

1. **Connect to a Wi-Fi network if you aren't already connected.**

   Creating a playlist requires a Wi-Fi connection because playlists are saved to the Cloud.

2. **Tap Create New Playlist.**

3. **In the screen that appears (see Figure 7-10), enter a playlist name and tap Save.**

   Kindle Fire HD displays a screen containing a Search field and a list of songs stored on the device.

4. **Tap the Add Song (+) button to the right of any song to select it.**

   If you've stored a lot of music and want to find a song without scrolling down the list, enter a song name in the Search field till the list narrows down to display it.

5. **Tap Done to save your playlist.**

   The Playlist is displayed (see Figure 7-11) and includes an Edit button that you can tap to edit the playlist contents.

Figure 7-9: The items you buy and download can be stored in playlists.

You can play the newly created playlist by simply tapping the Playlist tab, tapping the list you want to play, and then tapping the song you want to play.

When you tap the Edit button on a playlist, you see an Add Songs button and a Done button in the Edit screen. Songs appear with a Delete (–) symbol next to them; tap this symbol to delete a song. Tap the Add Song button to choose more songs to add to the playlist. Finally, tap Done when you're done editing.

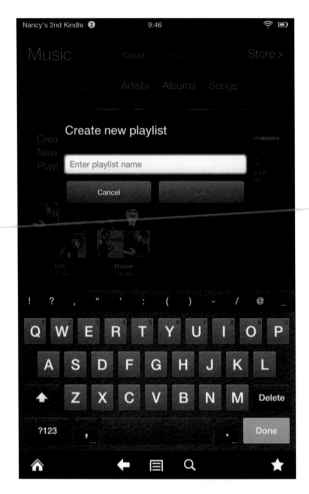

Figure 7-10: Assign a descriptive name for your playlist.

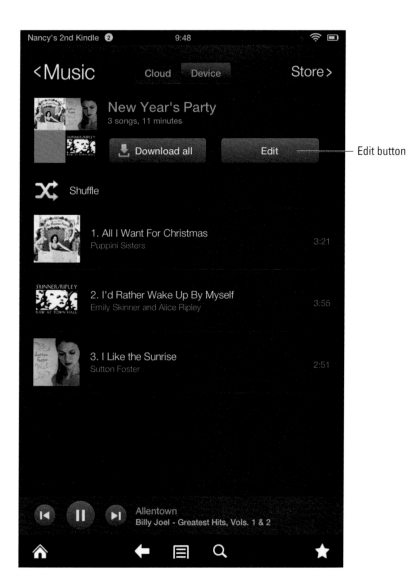

Edit button

Figure 7-11: A saved playlist.

8

Playing Video

*P*laying video, both movies and TV shows, is a great use of Kindle Fire HD. The device has a bright, crisp screen, can easily be held in one hand, and is capable of streaming video from the Amazon Cloud, making for a typically seamless viewing experience without hogging memory on the tablet itself.

In addition, Amazon offers an amazing selection of video content, including absolutely free Prime Instant Videos (as long as you maintain a Prime account with Amazon beyond the free 30 days that comes with the device).

You can discover the ins and outs of buying video content in Chapter 4. In this chapter, I explain how Amazon streams video content from the Cloud to your device, give you a look at the Kindle Fire HD Videos library, and cover the steps involved in playing a video. In addition, I introduce you to the X-Ray for Movies feature that makes use of the Amazon-owned IMDb movie database to provide background info on many videos as you watch.

Streaming versus Downloading

When you tap the Video button on the Kindle Fire HD Home screen, you're immediately taken to the Amazon Videos Store (see Figure 8-1), rather than to a library of video titles. That makes sense because, by design, Kindle

Fire HD is best used to stream videos from the Cloud rather than play them from a library on the device. The device's relatively small memory (16 or 32GB depending on the model you own) can't accommodate a large number of video files, so instead, Amazon makes it easy for you to stream video to the device without ever downloading it. To go to your Videos library, all you have to do is tap the Library button in the top-right corner.

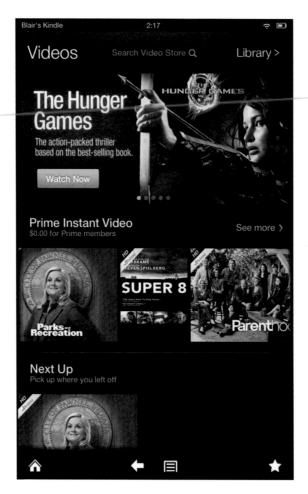

Figure 8-1: The Amazon Videos Store offers thousands of titles.

Video content in the Videos Store might include Prime Instant Videos (see Figure 8-2), a feature which offers thousands of titles for free with an Amazon Prime account. (If you don't already have an Amazon Prime account you get one free month of Amazon Prime with your Kindle Fire HD, after which you can purchase a membership for $79 a year.) You can also purchase or rent other video programs and stream them from the Cloud.

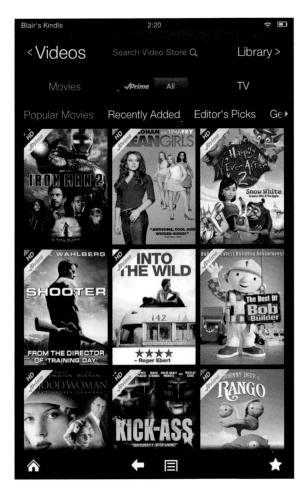

Figure 8-2: Browse thousands of free titles in the Prime Instant Videos section of the Videos Store.

Amazon's Whispersync technology keeps track of the spot in a video where you stopped watching on any device. You can later resume watching that video at that exact location on Kindle Fire HD, a PC or Mac, or one of over 300 compatible TVs, Blu-ray Disc players, or other devices.

You *can* download videos you purchase (you can't download Prime Instant Videos, however), which is useful if you want to watch them away from a Wi-Fi connection. It's a good idea to remove them from the device when you're done to save space. To delete a video from your device, open the Videos library and tap the Device tab. Press and hold your finger on the video, and then tap Remove from Device in the menu that appears.

Looking at Your Videos Library

I'm betting a lot of you are going to find that viewing video one-on-one on your Kindle Fire HD is a great way to get your entertainment. The Kindle Fire HD Videos library may become your favorite destination for buying, viewing, and organizing your video content.

When you tap Video on your Kindle Fire HD Home screen, the Amazon Videos Store opens (refer to Figure 8-1).

The Store shows several video categories in rows running down the screen such as Featured Videos, Prime Instant Videos, and Your Watchlist (Watchlist is a way to make note of items you may want to watch in the future; you can add any video to your Watchlist by tapping and holding it in the Store and then tapping Add to Watchlist in the menu that appears). Tap any video in the various lists to get more details about it.

When you tap the Prime Instant Videos category (refer to Figure 8-2), on the screen that appears, you can also use the tabs at the top of the screen to display just Movies, Prime, TV, or All Videos. There are also several tabs for narrowing your search such as Popular Movies, New Releases, Genres, or Editor's Picks (shown in Figure 8-3). The categories may change over time, but the basic process of locating a selection and displaying its details should stay the same.

When you tap the All button in the Store, you see all items across categories organized by popularity.

Tap the Library button to go to your Videos library (see Figure 8-4). The library sports two tabs — one lists all your videos stored in the Cloud, and one includes videos you've purchased that you have downloaded to the device. The tab that has orange lettering is the active tab.

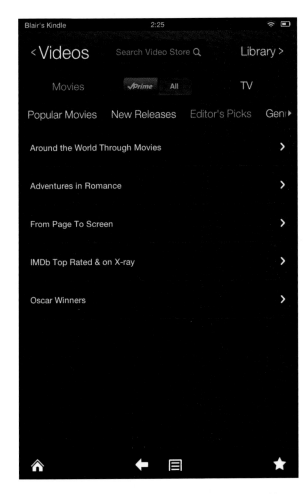

Figure 8-3: See what editors choose as their favorite videos in the Videos Store.

In addition to the Cloud and Device tabs, there are two tabs for filtering content by Movies or TV programs. You can tap the Search button in the Options bar (on the right side of the screen when the Kindle Fire HD is in landscape orientation) to search for a particular video.

Downloaded video content is listed chronologically by the date you downloaded it.

Figure 8-4: The Kindle Fire HD Videos library stored in the Amazon Cloud.

Tap the Menu button on the Options bar to display two items — Settings and Help & Feedback. In Settings you can view the Device ID and tap HD Download Options to access the Ask When Downloading setting (see Figure 8-5). If you disable this, it turns off a feature that asks you first before downloading high-definition videos. Though it's a good idea to be selective about downloading HD videos as they can take up a lot of memory, you may grow tired of seeing the message every time you download your new favorite flick.

Figure 8-5: Check out options for downloading HD and SD videos here.

You can tap the Menu button in the Options bar and then tap Your Watchlist to view the videos you've set aside in a list for future viewing.

Opening and Playing a Video

Playing a video is a simple process. If the video has been downloaded to your device, open the library (tap Videos, and then tap the Library button), locate the video (using methods described in the preceding section), and then tap the video to play it. If you've played the video before, you may have to tap a Resume, Start Over, or Download button to get it going again (see Figure 8-6).

Figure 8-6: Start again or resume where you left off.

If you're streaming a video that's stored in the Cloud for the first time, follow these steps:

1. **On the Kindle Fire HD's Home screen, tap Videos.**

2. **Tap the Library button in the top-right corner of the screen.**

3. **Tap the Cloud tab.**

   Videos you've rented (whose rental period hasn't expired) or purchased are displayed.

4. **Tap an item to open it.**

   If it's a TV show, you see episodes listed (see Figure 8-7); tap one to open it or tap the Buy button to buy an entire season. If it's a movie, at this point, you see a description of the movie and the option of watching it or downloading it (see Figure 8-8).

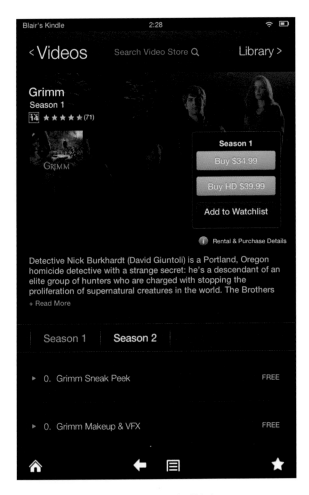

Figure 8-7: The episode list for a grim TV show.

5. **Tap the Watch Now button.**

The playback controls appear.

6. **If you've already watched part of the video, tap the Resume button (see Figure 8-6).**

If you'd rather see a video you've previously watched from its start, tap the Play from Beginning button.

The video appears full screen (see Figure 8-9). The title of the Movie appears at the bottom of the screen.

Figure 8-8: A new movie to watch!

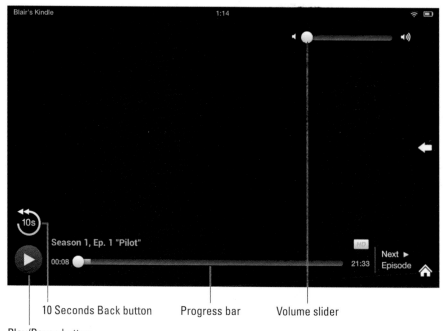

10 Seconds Back button   Progress bar   Volume slider

Play/Pause button

Figure 8-9: A movie with playback controls on Kindle Fire HD.

Note that the Kindle Fire HD screen provides an extra-wide viewing angle. This means that you and those watching with you (well, maybe one person watching with you — it does have a 7-inch or 8.9-inch screen, after all) can see the content from the side as well as from straight on.

The familiar playback tools available here include

- ✔ Play
- ✔ Pause
- ✔ A progress bar
- ✔ A volume slider
- ✔ A button that includes 10S in a circle that moves you ten seconds back in the video
- ✔ In the case of TV shows, a Next Episode button.

There's also a Back button in the Options bar that you can tap to stop playback and return to the Kindle Fire HD Videos library.

When you display a video's details in the Amazon Videos Store, you can tap the Rental & Purchase Details link to view the terms of use for playing the video.

Using X-Ray for Movies

When Kindle Fire HD arrived, so did the X-Ray feature. This feature works with some books and movies to give you access to facts about what you're reading or watching. This feature is based in part on the IMDb database of movie trivia, which Amazon, coincidentally, owns.

In the case of movies, the X-Ray feature provides information about the cast (see Figure 8-10) and if you tap on a particular cast member, you get details about that person's career and other movies he or she has appeared in (Figure 8-11).

To display X-Ray information, all you have to do is tap the screen when a movie is playing and the cast list appears in the top-left corner. Tap See Full Cast List to see the entire list and then tap on one to see details like those shown in Figure 8-11.

When you move a video to front and center on the Carousel, in the Customers Also Bought area at the bottom of the home screen there's an X-Ray item on the far left. Tap this to get X-Ray facts about the featured movie.

Figure 8-10: Find out more about the cast while watching the movie.

Figure 8-11: If you like the star, look for other movies featuring her here.

9

Going Social

In This Chapter

▷ Working with the Contacts app

▷ Utilizing integrated Facebook features

▷ Conducting video calls with Skype

K indle Fire HD isn't just about reading books, watching movies, and play-ing music. There are several ways in which you can use the device to interact and communicate with others.

In this chapter, I help you explore how Kindle Fire HD helps you keep in touch with people using the pre-installed Contacts app. I also explore how Kindle Fire HD integrates with Facebook and Twitter. Finally, I tell you all about using the Skype app and the new Kindle Fire HD camera and microphones to make video calls over the Internet.

Managing Contacts

The Contacts app pre-installed on Kindle Fire HD is a basic but useful contact management tool. You can enter or import contact information, sort that information by several criteria, and use Contacts to address e-mails.

You can find Contacts by tapping the Apps button on the Kindle Fire HD's Home screen. Tap the Contacts app to display its main screen, as shown in Figure 9-1.

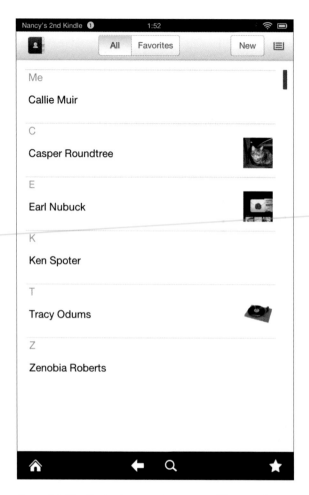

Figure 9-1: The Contacts app main screen with several contacts entered.

Importing contacts

If you have associated an e-mail account with your Kindle Fire HD, you can import all contacts from that account instead of entering each contact's information individually. (See Chapter 5 for more about setting up an e-mail provider account to sync with your Kindle Fire HD.)

After you have set up an associated e-mail account, when you first open Contacts and tap the New button, you get a message like that shown in Figure 9-2. Tap the account from which you want to import contacts. Your contacts are imported.

Figure 9-2: Synchronize to import contacts from your e-mail account.

If you want to create a new account you can tap the Add New Account button at this point. If you want to add another account from within Contacts at a later time, tap the Menu button in the top-right corner of Contacts, tap Settings, and then tap Add Account.

Creating new contacts

It's data entry time! Importing contacts (see the preceding section) is a nice shortcut, but you still need to know how to manually enter contacts by adding their information in the New Contact form.

To create a new contact, follow these steps:

1. **Tap the Contact app on the Carousel or in the Apps library to open it and then tap the New button to create a new contact.**

   The New Contact screen that appears (see Figure 9-3) contains fields including First Name, Last Name, Phone, and so on.

2. **Tap in a field and enter text.**

   The onscreen keyboard appears when you tap in a field.

3. **When you're done entering text in one field, tap the Next button on the onscreen keyboard to go to the next field.**

   Be sure to scroll to the bottom and enter detailed address information. You can tap Add Another Field at the bottom of the form to choose additional information fields to include.

4. **Tap the Photo icon at the top of the form and then tap Add Photo to add a photo.**

   Options appear for selecting photos as shown in Figure 9-4.

5. **Tap a photo source such as Photos to open it, double-tap to open a photo album; then tap a photo to add it to the contact record.**

6. **Tap Save.**

   The contact information displays as shown in Figure 9-5.

To edit the contact, tap the Edit button. To display all contacts, tap the All button. To delete the contact, tap the Delete button.

Viewing contacts

You can use settings to control how your contacts are organized and even save contacts to a list of Favorites in the Contacts app.

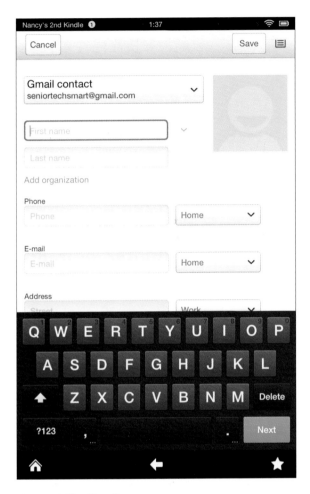

Figure 9-3: The New Contact screen.

To sort your contacts, follow these steps:

1. **On the bar across the top of the Contacts list, tap the Menu button and then tap Settings.**

   The E-Mail, Contacts, and Calendar settings appear.

2. **Tap Contacts General Settings.**

3. **Tap Sort Order of Contact Name to display the options shown in Figure 9-6.**

4. **Tap to sort by first name or last name.**

Figure 9-4: The photo Gallery may contain several albums.

You can also choose to view contacts in the Favorites area of the Home screen. To add a contact to Favorites, follow these steps:

1. **Tap Apps on the Kindle Fire HD's Home screen and then tap Contacts.**

   The Contacts app opens.

2. **Tap the All tab.**

3. **Tap the contact name you want to make a favorite.**

Figure 9-5: A contact record with photo included.

4. **Tap the star that appears next to the contact's name, as shown in Figure 9-7.**

   The star turns blue, indicating this is a favorite.

5. **Tap the Back arrow in the Options bar to display all contacts.**

6. **Tap the Favorites tab to display just contacts you've saved to Favorites.**

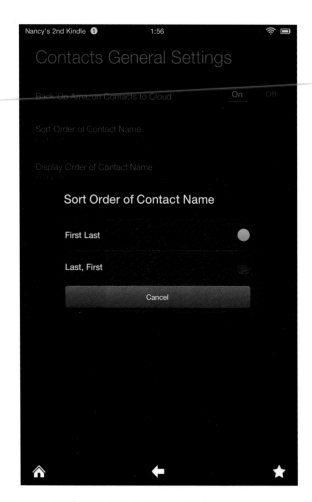

Figure 9-6: Choose from these basic sorting options.

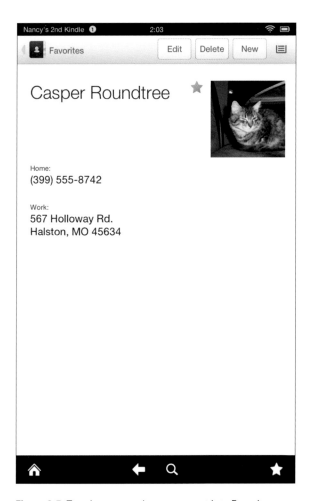

Figure 9-7: Tap the star to place a contact into Favorites.

Using Integrated Facebook and Twitter

If you want to work with your Facebook and Twitter accounts from your Kindle Fire HD, you can download those free apps from the Amazon Appstore. However, in order to share items via Facebook and Twitter, you can use integrated tools in Kindle Fire HD itself.

For example, if you're reading a book in your library, you can tap the screen to display tools and then tap the Share button at the top of the screen. This offers you the options shown in Figure 9-8 which lists shared comments from others on the same book. Simply enter a comment. If you want to share via Facebook or Twitter, just tap one of those options (refer to Figure 9-8) and a screen like the one shown in Figure 9-9 appears. Tap Connect and sign into your account to post your comment to your Facebook page or Twitter account.

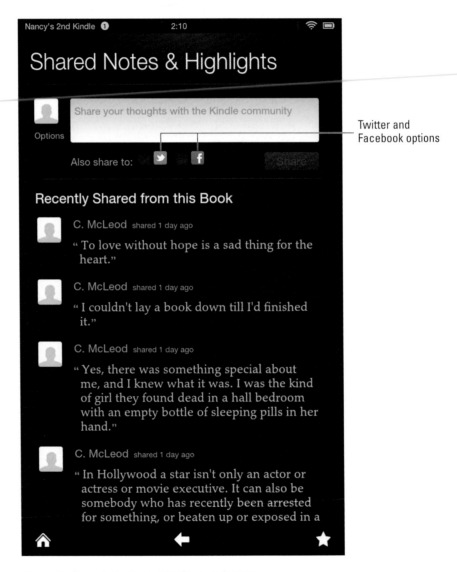

Twitter and Facebook options

Figure 9-8: Share comments with others on Amazon.

You can also compare your game progress with Facebook friends when you join GameCircle. When you tap the Games library on the Home screen, you see a screen such as the one shown in Figure 9-10. Tap the Connect button and you can create a connection between your Amazon account and Facebook. (Alternately, while in Games, if you have shared your GameCircle nickname by tapping the Show button, you can then tap the Menu button on the Options bar, then tap Settings and tap the On button to activate the link from Amazon to Facebook, as shown in Figure 9-11). You can then share you scores and achievements on Facebook and add any Facebook friends who have joined GameCircle.

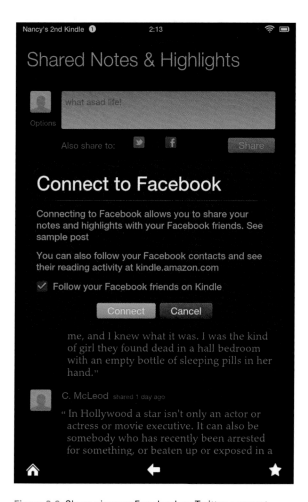

Figure 9-9: Share via your Facebook or Twitter account.

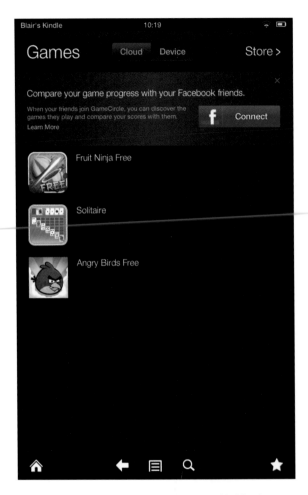

Figure 9-10: Compare your game progress with friends on Facebook.

Figure 9-11: Turn on Facebook for GameCircle here.

Making Calls with Skype

With Kindle Fire HD comes a camera and microphone that don't allow you to take photos or videos. What they do allow you to do is to make video calls to others using the popular Skype app, for which you may already have an account. The Skype app for Kindle Fire HD is free, but you will have to download it from the Amazon Appstore (see Chapter 4 for more about getting apps).

When you have downloaded the app, tap Apps from the Home Screen and then follow these steps:

1. **Tap the Skype app to open it. On the Welcome to Skype screen, tap Continue, and tap Accept on the following screen to accept terms and conditions.**

2. **In the screen shown in Figure 9-12, enter a Skype Name and Password.**

   If you've never created a Skype account, tap the Create an Account button at this point and enter your name, Skype Name, a password, e-mail address, and phone number to create your Skype account.

3. **Tap the Sign In button and, on the following screen, tap Continue.**

   On the screen that appears (see Figure 9-13), you can tap on three options to make calls:

   - **Contacts:** This displays a list of contacts saved in your Kindle Fire HD's Contacts app. Tap one and then tap the Call button (it's green with a little phone handset in it, as shown in Figure 9-14) to place a call.

   - **Recent:** This displays recently made calls so you can tap on one to call the person again.

   - **Call Phones:** This displays the screen shown in Figure 9-15. Enter the number you want to call in the field at the top of the screen and then tap the Call button to place the call.

Figure 9-12: If you have a Skype account, enter your information here.

Figure 9-13: The main Skype screen offers several ways to place calls.

Call button

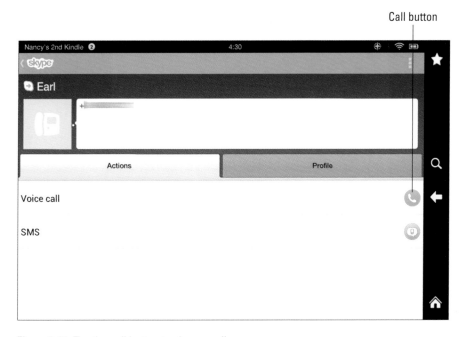

Figure 9-14: Tap the call button to place a call.

Here are a few more tips to remember about using Skype on your Kindle Fire HD:

✔ You need to have credits to call people who aren't Skype users. Go to www.skype.com and sign in with your account information to buy credits.

✔ From the Skype main screen on Kindle Fire HD, you can tap the Profile button and enter a message that's shared with all of your contacts, such as the phone number you use to accept Skype calls.

Figure 9-15: Enter any number here and place your call.

✔ You can tap the Status icon (a small white box with a check mark in it; refer to Figure 9-13) to indicate that you're online, away, or unavailable to callers.

✔ You can tap the Menu button (it looks like three vertical dots) in the top-right corner of the Skype app main screen and then tap the Settings option to access settings for receiving incoming calls, syncing contacts, signing in automatically, and so on, as shown in Figure 9-16.

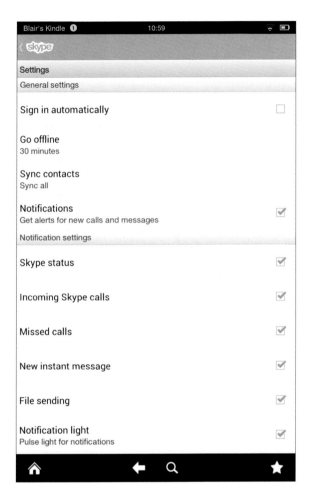

Figure 9-16: You can control your incoming and outgoing call experience with these settings.

10

Getting Productive with Kindle Fire HD

*K*indle Fire HD isn't just about watching movies and playing music. There are several ways in which you can use the device to get your work done and share documents and images with others.

In this chapter, I help you explore how Kindle Fire HD helps you view and share documents. The new pre-installed Calendar app is useful for keeping on schedule, and it's covered in this chapter. If you need to view or edit photos for work or play, here's where you get to explore what the simple Photos app has to offer. And finally, I show you the easy-to-use features that make the free *New Oxford American Dictionary* a very useful tool for the writer in you.

Understanding Kindle Docs

One of the items you see across the top of your Kindle Fire HD Home screen is the Docs library (see Figure 10-1). Documents will be stored in the Docs library, to which this button provides access, and if you've viewed them recently, they may also be available on the Carousel. You can also save docs to Favorites on the Home screen (see Chapter 2 for more about Favorites) or upload docs from your computer to the Amazon Cloud.

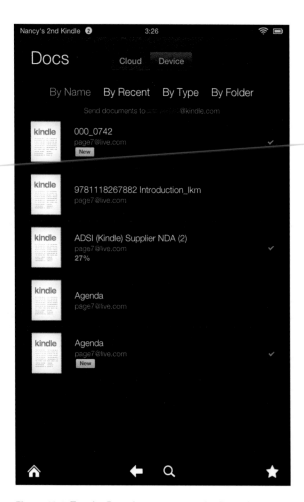

Figure 10-1: Tap the Docs button to open the Docs library.

In the following sections, you can discover how docs get onto your Kindle Fire HD and how you can view and share them. I also provide some advice about using productivity software on Kindle Fire HD to get your work done.

Getting docs onto Kindle Fire HD

Documents help you communicate information in forms ranging from news-letters to memos and garage sale flyers to meeting agendas.

To get a doc onto your Kindle Fire HD, you can *sideload* (transfer) it from your PC or Mac by using the Micro USB cable that comes with Kindle Fire HD or e-mailing it to yourself at your Kindle e-mail address (locate this address by opening your Docs library; it's listed below the sort tabs — By Name, By Recent, and so on — near the top of the screen).

Documents come in different formats. Some formats come from the originat-ing software, such as Microsoft Word. Other formats can be opened by a vari-ety of software programs, such as RTF documents that can be opened by any word processor program. In Kindle Fire HD, supported document formats include TXT, Microsoft Word DOCX, HTML, RTF, or PDF, as well as Amazon's Mobi or ASW formats. Some documents will be converted to one of these Amazon formats automatically.

If you send a document to your Kindle e-mail address, the file appears in your Docs library automatically. You can also get a variety of common graphic file formats onto Kindle Fire HD which will be stored in your Photos app. Kindle Fire HD even supports compressed (Zip) file formats and automatically unzips them when they're transferred to your device via e-mail.

Although you can view these documents, as shown in Figures 10-2 and 10-3, at this point in time, you can't edit them on your Kindle Fire HD without downloading an app such as OfficeSuite Pro.

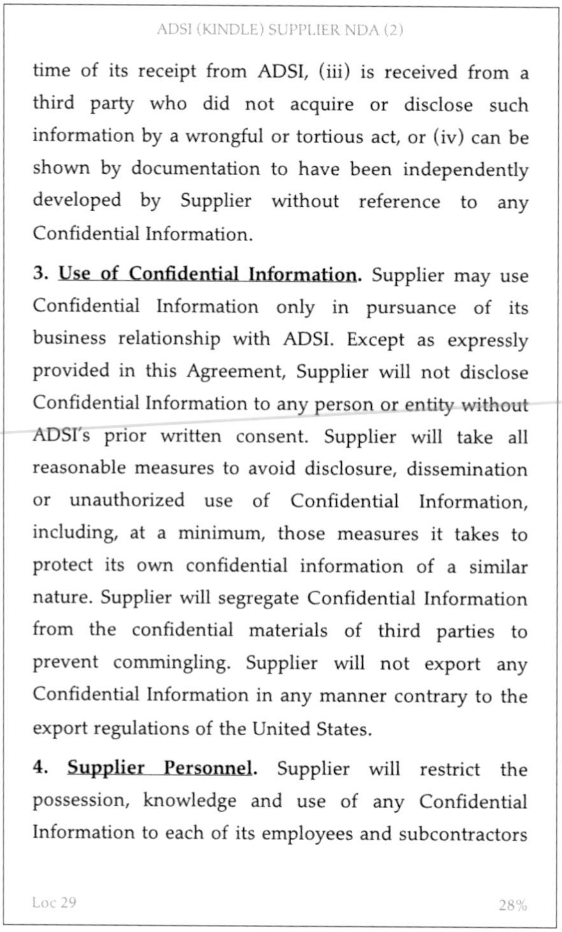

ADSI (KINDLE) SUPPLIER NDA (2)

time of its receipt from ADSI, (iii) is received from a third party who did not acquire or disclose such information by a wrongful or tortious act, or (iv) can be shown by documentation to have been independently developed by Supplier without reference to any Confidential Information.

3. Use of Confidential Information. Supplier may use Confidential Information only in pursuance of its business relationship with ADSI. Except as expressly provided in this Agreement, Supplier will not disclose Confidential Information to any person or entity without ADSI's prior written consent. Supplier will take all reasonable measures to avoid disclosure, dissemination or unauthorized use of Confidential Information, including, at a minimum, those measures it takes to protect its own confidential information of a similar nature. Supplier will segregate Confidential Information from the confidential materials of third parties to prevent commingling. Supplier will not export any Confidential Information in any manner contrary to the export regulations of the United States.

4. Supplier Personnel. Supplier will restrict the possession, knowledge and use of any Confidential Information to each of its employees and subcontractors

Loc 29   28%

Figure 10-2: A Word document displayed on Kindle Fire HD.

To sideload docs to your Kindle Fire HD, grab the Micro USB cable that came with Kindle Fire HD, and then follow these steps:

1. **Attach the Micro USB end of the cable to your Kindle Fire HD.**

2. **Attach the USB end of the cable to your computer.**

   Your Kindle Fire HD will appear as a drive in Windows Explorer on a Windows computer or the Mac Finder on a Mac (see Figure 10-4).

Acme Marine Supply

1234 Spring Street

Lost Harbor, WA 98838

May 23, 2013

To Whom It May Concern:

Arlene Smith was an employee of our company from June 2010 to April 2013. In her duties Arlene was a
fine employee who was diligent and hard working.

Arlene asked us to write a letter of recommendation to your school. We consider her to be of very good
character, very intelligent and responsible, and she would be an asset to your student body. Please
contact us if you would like any further information about her.

Sincerely,

John Randall

Store Manager

360 555-0099

Figure 10-3: A PDF document displayed on Kindle Fire HD.

3. **Click the appropriate choice to open and view files on the drive that appears (see Figure 10-5).**

4. **Double-click the Internal Storage folder and then click and drag files from your hard drive to the Docs folder in the Kindle Fire HD window.**

   You can also copy and paste documents from one drive to the other. Drag documents to the Documents folder, pictures to the Photos folder, audio files to the Music folder, and so on.

5. **Tap the Disconnect button on your Kindle Fire HD to safely eject the Kindle Fire HD from your computer.**

Figure 10-4: Options for opening up content of Kindle Fire HD.

Figure 10-5: Your Kindle Fire HD appears like an external drive on your computer when attached using a Micro USB cable.

You can now unplug the Micro USB cord from your Kindle Fire HD and computer.

Docs are only stored on your Kindle Fire HD, not backed up to the Amazon Cloud. If you want to back up documents, use the Micro USB cable to copy them back to your computer.

Opening docs

After you put a doc onto your Kindle Fire HD by either sideloading it from a computer or receiving it through Kindle e-mail, you can view the document by following these steps:

1. **Tap the Docs button on the Kindle Fire HD Home screen to open the Docs library.**

   Alternatively, you can locate recently viewed docs on the Carousel and docs you've saved to Favorites in the Favorites area of the Home screen.

2. **When the library opens (see Figure 10-6), tap a tab to see the library contents.**

   You can choose one of three categories: By Name, By Recent, or By Type. If you are looking at docs in your Amazon Cloud account, you can also view them By Folder; you can create folders from the Amazon Cloud site.

3. **When you find the document you want to view, tap the arrow to the right of it to open it.**

At this point in time, you can view only documents, and with Word format documents, you can add notes and highlights. However, you can't edit them at all without a third-party app.

To search for a document, tap the Search button in the Options bar, type a document name in the Search field; tap a tab to search from among Libraries, Stores, or Web; and tap Go on the onscreen keyboard.

E-mailing docs

When you have a doc on your Kindle Fire HD, you can view it and also share it with others as an e-mail attachment. Follow these steps to attach a doc to an e-mail message:

1. **Tap the Favorites button on the Home screen.**

   A list of favorite installed apps appears. If you've removed the E-mail app from your Favorites, look for it by tapping the Apps library.

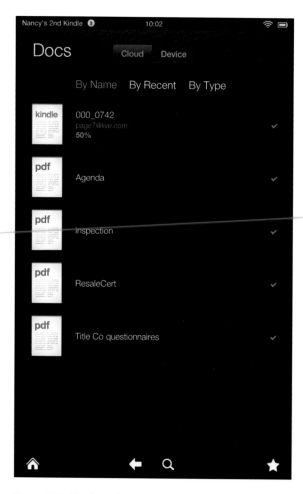

Figure 10-6: The Docs library with tabs by category.

2. **Tap the E-mail app.**

   The E-mail app opens.

3. **Tap your Inbox and then tap the New button (see Figure 10-7).**

   A blank e-mail form appears, as shown in Figure 10-8.

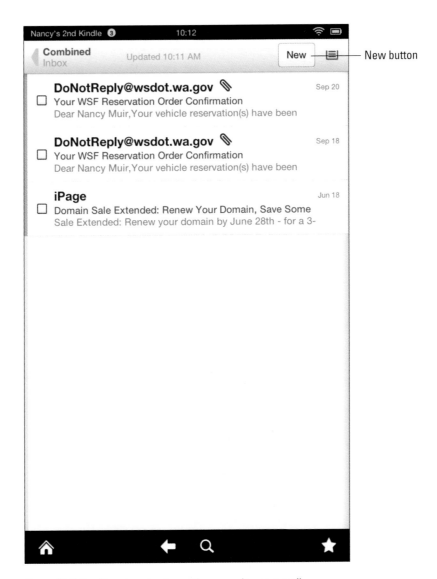

Figure 10-7: Tap New to get going with composing an e-mail.

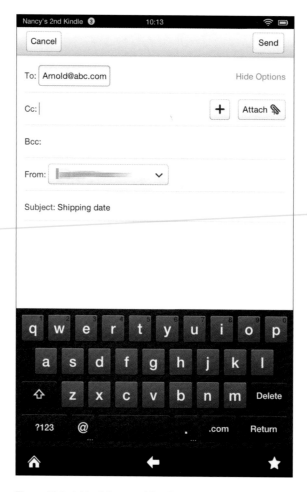

Figure 10-8: A blank form waiting for you to enter an e-mail address, subject, and message.

4. **Enter a name in the To field, a subject, and a message.**

5. **Tap Options and then tap the Attach button, shown in the top-right portion of the screen in Figure 10-8.**

   In the menu that appears (see Figure 10-9), choose to attach an item from the Photos or Videos apps, or from OfficeSuite. If you choose OfficeSuite, you can then tap on the My Documents folder to access all the documents in your Docs app. You can also choose Internal Storage which will include folders for various libraries, including Music, Books, and Docs.

6. **Tap Send.**

   Your document goes on its way, attached to your e-mail.

Figure 10-9: Attaching a doc to an e-mail message.

Taking documents further

If you want to do more than view documents on your Kindle Fire HD, consider using the built-in app called OfficeSuite (see Figure 10-10). This productivity suite for Android gives you the ability to view (but not edit) word processor, spreadsheet, and presentation files.

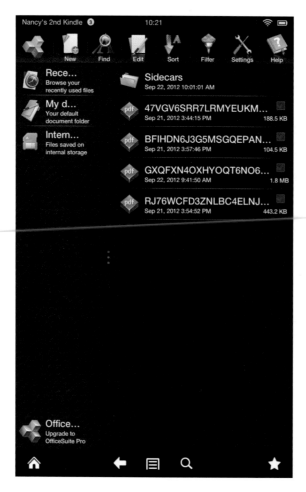

Figure 10-10: The various pieces of OfficeSuite are available from this opening page.

Another option you can check out is OfficeSuite Pro (see Figure 10-11), which will cost you $14.99 but lets you both view and edit Microsoft Word and Excel documents and view Microsoft PowerPoint files. If you open the OfficeSuite app that comes pre-installed on your Kindle Fire HD, you can tap on an Upgrade to OfficeSuite Pro icon in the lower-left corner to upgrade to the more robust app.

Also consider using an online productivity suite such as Google Docs (www. docs.google.com). This website offers hosted software you can use to create and edit documents online, and it's compatible with the Microsoft Office Suite. You can access such an online suite and work with online docs by using the Silk browser. See Chapter 5 for more about Silk.

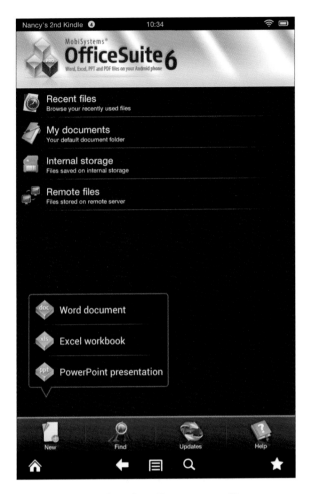

Figure 10-11: OfficeSuite Pro offers common office productivity tools.

See Chapter 11 for a list of great apps you can get to flesh out your Kindle Fire HD functionality, such as calculator and note-taking apps.

Staying on Time with Calendar

The pre-installed Calendar app is new with Kindle Fire HD. The simple calendar interface, which you can display by day, week, or month, allows you to sync with calendars from your e-mail account and then view and edit events and create new events.

Calendar views

Before you can use many of Calendar's features, you have to sync it with a calendar account, typically through your e-mail provider. When you first open Calendar, you see the blank calendar shown in Figure 10-12.

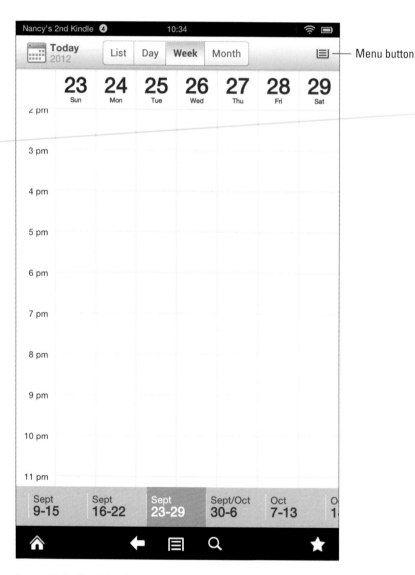

Menu button

Figure 10-12: The Calendar app is a welcome addition to Kindle Fire HD.

Tap on a tab to display the calendar by Day, Week, or Month, or to display a List of events. Note that if you tap on a date in the Month view, that date opens in Day view.

To move to other dates, use the buttons along the bottom of the screen (refer to Figure 10-12). In Day view, these buttons will be dates just before and after the currently displayed day; in Week view, the buttons will be labeled for weeks just before and after the current week; and in Month view, you tap on a button for another month.

Syncing with a calendar account

You can't add a new event until you sync with a calendar in an online account, so follow these steps to sync:

1. **Tap the Menu button (refer to Figure 10-12) and then tap the New Event option in the menu that appears.**

2. **Tap the Add Account button in the screen shown in Figure 10-13.**

3. **Tap an account in the list shown in Figure 10-14, such as AOL, Exchange, or Hotmail, or tap Other Provider for any other type of account.**

4. **On the following screen (see Figure 10-15), enter your account information and tap Next.**

   You may see a message about how POP access is required to get Plus features, if available, for your account.

5. **Tap OK to proceed.**

   Kindle Fire HD may take a few seconds to sync with your account. You return to the Calendar and can now add and edit events.

Create a new Calendar event

Events are brought over from the calendar you sync with, but you can also add new events. With either Day or Week view displayed, follow these steps to add an event:

Figure 10-13: Add an account to sync calendar events with.

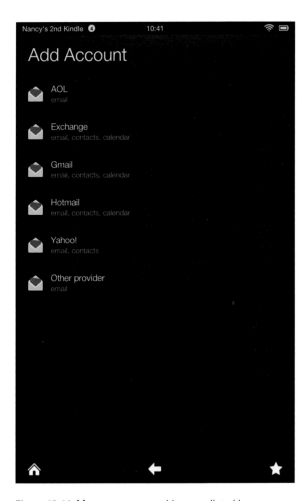

Figure 10-14: Most common providers are listed here.

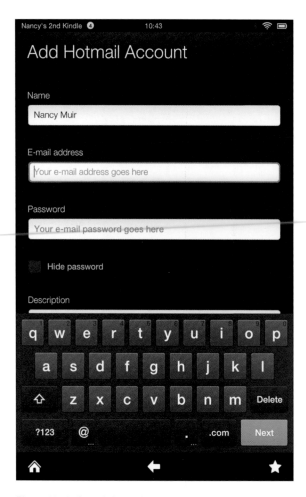

Figure 10-15: Enter information about the account you want to sync with Calendar.

1. **Tap on a date or time in the Week or Day calendar (depending on which view you're displaying) and then tap the New Event button that appears.**

   This button shows a plus sign (+) in Week view and the phrase +New Event in the Day view.

2. **The New Event form shown in Figure 10-16 appears.**

3. **Tap on the words New Event and enter a title for the event.**

Figure 10-16: Use this form to enter info for a new event.

4. **Tap in the From time and date fields and choose a start time and date, and then tap in the To time and date fields and choose an ending time and date.**

   If the event runs all day, skip the From and To field settings and simply tap the All Day check box.

5. **Tap the Repeat field if you want an event to repeat at a regular interval.**

   This setting is useful for events such as weekly company meetings, monthly get-togethers, or car or house maintenance items that are required on a regular basis, for example.

6. **You can tap the Reminders field to choose to get an alert on your Kindle Fire HD at a certain interval before the event commences.**

7. **If you want to invite a person you've saved as a contact, tap the plus sign (+) button in the Invite field.**

8. **If you wish, enter information in the Where and Notes fields.**

9. **Tap Save.**

   The event appears in your Calendar, as shown in Figure 10-17.

Figure 10-17: Here's your newly created event!

To edit an event, simply tap to open it and then tap the Edit button.

Viewing Photos

Kindle Fire HD has a pre-installed Photos app for all you photography lovers. Though its features are pretty basic, Photos allows you to view and do minor edits to photos.

Getting photos onto Kindle Fire HD

The Kindle Fire HD's camera can't capture photos, so you have to get photos onto the device by saving an image from the Internet using your Silk browser or copying them from your computer by using your Micro USB cable (see the section "Getting docs onto Kindle Fire HD," earlier in this chapter, for more about this procedure). Using this procedure, you can copy photos into the Pictures folder on your Kindle Fire HD by using Windows Explorer or the Mac Finder.

Viewing photos

After you load photos into your Pictures library and disconnect the Micro USB cable, you can tap the Photos app on the Home screen. This displays an album that represents the folder you copied to your Kindle Fire HD (see Figure 10-18) and other albums for other sources, such as for downloads and screenshots. If you copy another folder of photos, it will come over as a separate album. Photos in albums are organized chronologically by the date you placed them on your Kindle Fire HD.

There are three main actions you can perform to view pictures:

✔ Tap to open an album and view the pictures within it.

✔ Tap a picture to make it appear full screen.

✔ Swipe left or right to move through pictures in an album.

You can also tap the E-Mail button in the Options bar while in Photos to e-mail the displayed photo. Another method to share via e-mail is to tap the Options bar, tap Share, and then tap Send with Email. In the e-mail message that appears with the photo already attached, enter an address, subject, and message, and then tap the Send button.

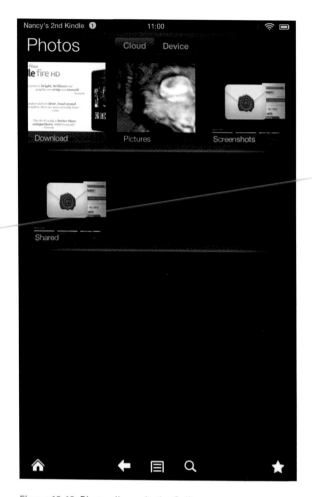

Figure 10-18: Photo albums in the Gallery.

Managing photos in the Amazon Cloud Drive

There are two things you can do to photos to manage them — move photos from one album to another and rename photos or photo albums:

- ✔ **Moving photos:** To move a photo, you need to go to the Amazon Cloud Drive using a browser (go to Amazon.com, tap or click Your Account, and then tap or click Your Cloud Drive on the list that appears; you will have to sign into your account at this point). Use the More Actions drop-down list and choose Move *X* Items To . . . (where *X* is the number of items you've selected) and then choose the folder on your Cloud Drive to move the item(s) to.

- ✔ **Rename:** You can rename a picture or albums from within Cloud Drive by tapping or clicking the More Actions button and then choosing Rename. You can also rename an album from your Kindle Fire HD in the Photos app by long-pressing (pressing and holding for a few seconds) the album and choosing Rename from the menu that appears.

You can click the New Folder button to add albums to help you organize your photos. Then use the Moving photos directions above to move photos into the album.

Note that when viewing photos on your Kindle Fire HD you can also enlarge or reduce a photo by pinching and unpinching with your fingers on the touchscreen.

When you display a photo full screen in the Photos app, you see tools at bottom of the screen, including Zoom In, Zoom Out, and a tool that causes the image to fit within the screen again if you've enlarged it.

With a photo displayed, if you want to delete it, simply tap the Trash button on the Options bar.

Using the New Oxford American Dictionary

If you tap the Books button and tap the Device tab, you'll see the *New Oxford American Dictionary, Second Edition*, in your book library. Amazon thought-fully provided this book to help you find your way with words.

In addition to being able to browse through the dictionary, when you press and hold a word in a book or magazine, a dictionary definition from the *New Oxford American Dictionary* is displayed (see Figure 10-19). You can tap the Full Definition button to go to the full dictionary entry.

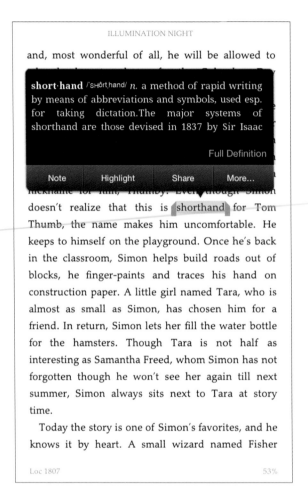

Figure 10-19: A definition displayed in an e-book.

When you open the dictionary, you can flick from page to page; entries are arranged here alphabetically, as with any dictionary. You can also use the Linked Entries links to go to related terms from any definition (see Figure 10-20).

As with any book, you can tap the Settings button on the tools at the top of the page to adjust font size, line spacing, margins, and the background color of the pages. You can also tap the Search button in the Options bar to locate a specific word, and tap the X-Ray button feature to get more information about the book (though at this time the dictionary says X-Ray concepts are "not yet available for this book").

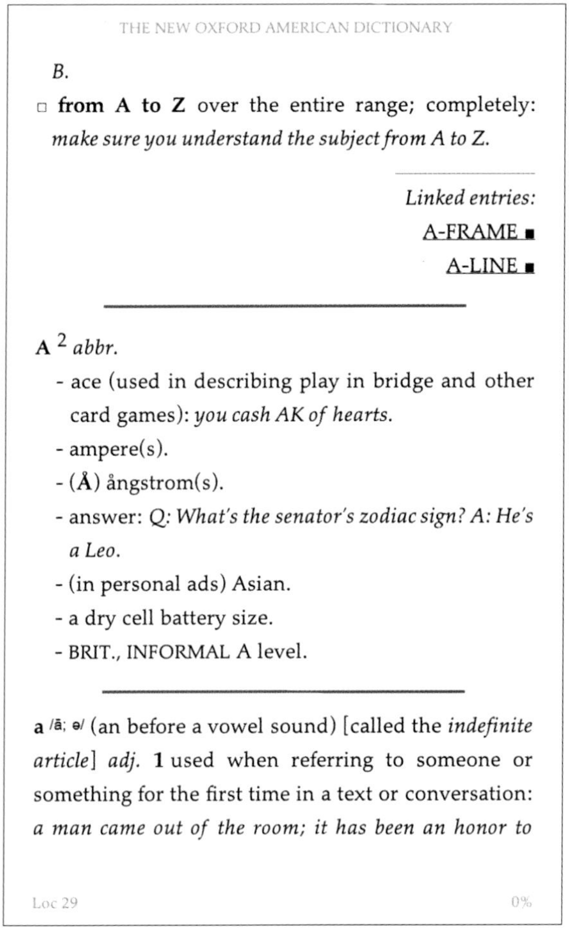

THE NEW OXFORD AMERICAN DICTIONARY

B.

☐ **from A to Z** over the entire range; completely: *make sure you understand the subject from A to Z.*

Linked entries:

A-FRAME ▪

A-LINE ▪

A ² *abbr.*

- ace (used in describing play in bridge and other card games): *you cash AK of hearts.*
- ampere(s).
- (Å) ångstrom(s).
- answer: *Q: What's the senator's zodiac sign? A: He's a Leo.*
- (in personal ads) Asian.
- a dry cell battery size.
- BRIT., INFORMAL A level.

a /ā; ə/ (an before a vowel sound) [called the *indefinite article*] *adj.* **1** used when referring to someone or something for the first time in a text or conversation: *a man came out of the room; it has been an honor to*

Loc 29   0%

Figure 10-20: Many entries have linked entries that provide related information.

That's about all there is to the dictionary, but it can prove to be a handy resource for those who love words.

See Chapter 6 for more about reading all kinds of e-books on Kindle Fire HD.

Keeping your finger on the Pulse

Another neat app you can use to enlighten yourself is Pulse News, a free news aggregator. This app allows you to choose from among various sources of content, such as *The New Yorker* or ESPN Headlines, and then access them from one central location. You can download the Pulse News app from the Amazon Appstore.

Part IV
The Part of Tens

The 5th Wave — By Rich Tennant

"Okay antidote, antidote, what would an antidote app look like? You know, I still haven't got this Home screen the way I'd like it."

In this part . . .

This part includes two chapters that recommend apps you can get to add basic functionality to the Kindle Fire HD, such as a calculator and notes, and ten games to turn your Kindle Fire HD into a great gaming machine.

11

Ten Apps That Add Functionality to Kindle Fire HD

*A*ny mobile device today, from a smartphone to a tablet, thrives on the thousands of apps that make a world of features available.

Kindle Fire HD has functionality built in for consuming books, periodicals, music, and video, as well as a contact management, calculator, and calendar app, web browser, and e-mail client. However, there are some tools that many of us have grown used to having available that you can easily acquire by adding apps to the device.

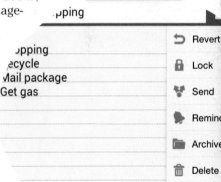

Amazon Appstore, which you learn the ins and outs of using in Chapter 4, contains thousands of cool apps for you to explore. To help you flesh out the basic tools in Kindle Fire HD, in this chapter, I provide reviews of apps such as a note taker, alarm, and unit converter that meet your day-to-day needs and whet your *app*etite. Most of these are free.

From a nutrition guide to a very cool drawing app, these will provide you fun and useful functionality for your Kindle Fire HD and not cost you much more than the time to download them.

SketchBook Mobile

From: AutoDesk, Inc.

Price: $1.99

SketchBook (see Figure 11-1) is a drawing app to satisfy the creative artist in your soul. With 47 preset brushes, you can draw whatever you can imagine on your Kindle Fire HD screen. You can control the brush characteristics and make use of an extensive color palette.

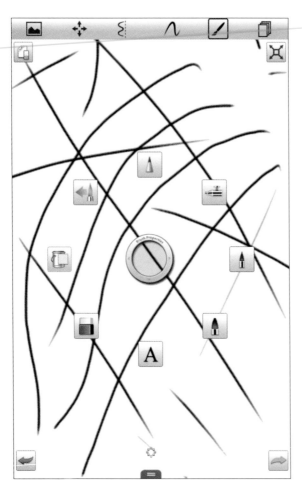

Figure 11-1: Sketchbook brings out the artist in you.

Try sideloading photos and modifying them with this clever app, then save your files in JPEG, PNG, or PSD formats. When you're done, it's easy to e-mail your artistic efforts to yourself to print from your computer.

The Brush Properties circular control lets you easily adjust the size and opacity of the writing tools. Touch the square at the top of the screen to access color controls and watch the Red, Blue, and Green levels adjust as you move around the color wheel.

However, be careful of the Erase button in the upper-left corner of the screen: I've erased more than one picture by tapping this when I shouldn't have!

Fast Food Nutrition Lite

From: FastFood.com

Price: Free

If you're watching your weight but are forced to scarf down fast food now and then, this little app could have an impact on your waistline. Not limited to traditional drive-thru fast food joints, the app gives you nutritional information about dishes from 100 restaurant chains, such as Applebees, Chili's, and Checker's, and includes over 25,000 menu items (see Figure 11-2).

Fast Food Nutrition Lite helps you keep track of calories, Weight Watchers points, fats, trans fats, saturated fats, cholesterol, sodium, carbohydrates, sugars, and protein. The calorie counter shows you how much of the recommended daily allowance each meal is providing you. Select the items you want in your meal and touch View Order, which displays a handy screen showing you all the totals for your meal.

You can add thumbnails for your favorite restaurants so that you don't have to search through all the restaurants to find the ones you like best.

You sometimes pay a price to get a free app. In the case of this app, and several others, that price is having to view ads as you use the app.

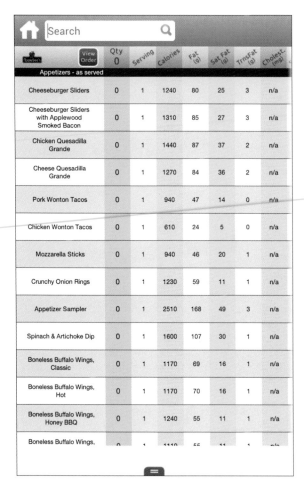

Figure 11-2: Keep track of your calories with this handy counter.

Alarm Clock Xtreme Free

From: Angle Labs, Inc.

Price: Free

Kindle Fire HD has no built-in alarm app, so this one is a natural to add to your apps collection. This easy-to-use alarm app can help keep you on schedule (see Figure 11-3). You can create and edit alarms and control how far ahead of events and at what intervals you're alerted to alarms.

Figure 11-3: Get alarms to get you going on time.

You can set a timer with this app and have the app display a countdown to the event (countdown to Christmas, countdown to your wedding day, your choice!). You can change the look and feel of the alarm app with different colored backgrounds and a large Snooze button.

Astral Budget

From: Astral Web, Inc.

Price: Free

If you're like many of us, these days, you're tightening your belt and counting those pennies. Astral Budget is an app that helps you keep track of all your expenses, whether for a single trip or your yearly household budget. You can use built-in categories for fixed spending such as rent, food, travel, utilities, and so on to categorize your expenses.

The app has four sections: Goals, Expense, Reports, and Export (see Figure 11-4). Using these, you can enter the amounts you want to spend and track them against actual expenditures. You can use the wide variety of Reports in Astral Budget to examine your spending trends and even export data to your computer to examine with the more-robust application Excel. I like the Chart selections, including bar charts, pie charts, and list charts.

Figure 11-4: Use various tools to enter and visualize your spending practices.

ColorNote Notepad Notes

From: Social & Mobile, Inc.

Price: Free

Kindle Fire HD also doesn't include a note-taking app, and if you're like me, you need one. If being able to keep a to-do list warms the cockles of your organized (or disorganized) heart, this is a neat little free app, and it's very simple to use.

You can keep a simple to-do list or other random notes, and even share information with your friends via e-mail, social networks, or messaging (honey, here's the shopping list for your evening commute!).

ColorNote allows some nice word-processing-like functions, such as the ability to edit and delete completed items from lists (see Figure 11-5).

You can even set up reminders for items in your notes and search for specific content.

If your notes are top secret, consider using the password feature in ColorNote.

Figure 11-5: When you finish an item on your list, delete it.

Cube Calculator

From: IP

Price: Free

It's a good idea to add a calculator to Kindle Fire HD, if only to figure out tips and your sales commissions, right? This is a calculator with tons of bells and whistles, from the ability to use mathematical expressions and time calculations to logarithmic and trigonometric functions.

Even if you're not a power math user, the very nice interface (see Figure 11-6) in this app makes casual calculations simple to do. Also, the help system for this app is actually helpful.

You can choose a theme such as Light or Dark to ease your eyestrain as you calculate. You can also control the maximum number of digits to be returned in a result (after all, who needs pi to go on ad infinitum?).

Figure 11-6: The keyboard sports bold fonts and is easy to use.

Handrite Note Pro

From: Ben Lee

Price: $2.99

If you miss the feeling of writing notes by hand, instead of typing them on plastic keyboards, this app is for you. It's simple to use: Tap to create a new note, and then use the spiral-bound pad interface to write words or draw images on the page with your finger. You can change the stroke width and text size for your writing and even use different colors (see Figure 11-7).

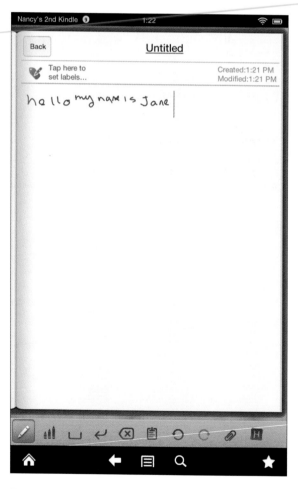

Figure 11-7: Writing on your Kindle Fire HD screen is very freeing.

When you close the app, your note is saved, but you can press and hold the touchscreen to edit the text you entered. You can also create a label for a note and export it. The app isn't fancy; it's more for jotting down a phone number when you see a flyer about a missing kitten or making a quick note to yourself about what to pick up at the store, but for what it is, it's darn handy and easy to use.

Exchange by TouchDown

From: NitroDesk, Inc.

Price: Free

If you want to access e-mail, contacts, and calendar information from your workplace and your company uses Microsoft Exchange Server for these accounts, this little app will help you tap into your company e-mail. It touts itself as providing great security and provides the very handy service of wiping data from your Kindle Fire HD remotely if it's lost or stolen.

Keep in mind that TouchDown doesn't work with IMAP or POP3 servers; it's intended for Exchange Servers, as well as supporting Zimbra, Kerio, and ActiveSync. Though the app has pretty-easy-to-use settings (see Figure 11-8), you might want to sit down over a cup of coffee with your network administrator to get this one working. But when you do, I think you'll be pleased.

Figure 11-8: Make settings yourself or enlist the aid of your administrator.

Units

From: staticfree.info

Price: Free

If, like me, you need help converting just about anything to anything else (feet to meters, pounds to kilos, or whatever), you'll appreciate this handy little app. It handles 2,400 different conversions, including height, weight, volume, volume to weight, and time to distance. Tap the Unit key, and you'll see a list of the various types of conversions available (see Figure 11-9).

Just fill in the You Have field and the You Want field, and then enter the number of units. Tap the equal sign (=) and get your conversion. Holding Kindle Fire HD in landscape orientation displays a few more helpful tools on the calculator-style interface.

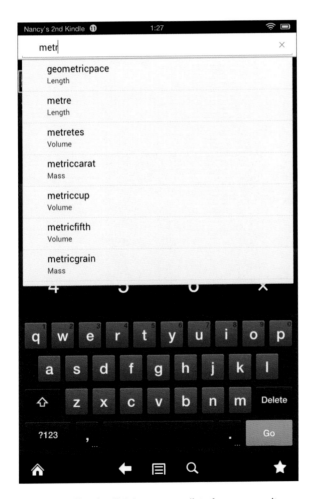

Figure 11-9: Tap the Unit key to get a list of common units.

Wi-Fi Analyzer

From: farproc

Price: Free

Because Kindle Fire HD can connect to the web only through Wi-Fi, with the exception of the model that can use 4G LTE to connect, this handy app is helpful for keeping track of local Wi-Fi connections. You can observe available Wi-Fi channels and the signal strength on each (see Figure 11-10). There are several styles of graph to choose from, including Channel, Time, Channel Rating, and Signal Meter.

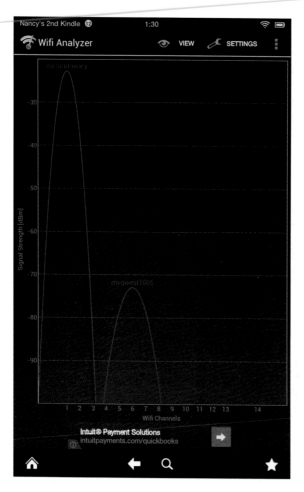

Figure 11-10: Figure out whether your nearest Wi-Fi will help you connect.

12

Ten (or So) Top Gaming Apps

*P*eople using tablets will tell you that one of the great uses for them is to play games of all sorts. From card games such as solitaire to graphically entertaining new classics like Asphalt 7: Heat and Fruit Ninja, having access to games helps you while away a quiet evening at home or keep yourself from getting bored in boring settings, such as the security line at the airport or the dentist's waiting room.

Be sure to check out GameCircle, Amazon's new combination of social networking and gaming. Open the Games library and tap Connect to connect through Facebook and find friends who are using Amazon GameCircle. You can then share scores, achievements, and the games that you love to play with others.

In this chapter, I introduce you to 11 great games that will provide hours of fun and create the core of your Kindle Fire gaming library.

Cut the Rope

From: Zepto Lab

Price: $0.99

This is a very addictive game (ask my husband, I'm a Cut the Rope widow). The whole idea is that there's this monster you have to feed candy (don't ask why). The candy swings on ropes (see Figure 12-1), and you have to figure out how to cut the rope so the candy whacks into various star-shaped objects, exploding them, and eventually ends up in the monster's mouth.

Along the way, you encounter various devices, such as little air blowers or balloons that help you manipulate items on the screen and achieve your goals. Of course, you'll want to turn off the annoying music and little sounds that seem to come from the candy. In the Menu setting on the Options bar, tap the little speaker to mute the sound. Then, have fun feeding the monster!

Figure 12-1: Figure out which rope to cut to whack the stars and feed the monster.

Plants vs. Zombies

From: PopCap Games, Inc.

Price: $2.99

If you're somebody who worries about zombies attacking your home (and who doesn't?), this game will appeal to you. A phalanx of zombies waits on the street outside your house. You get to put plants in your front lawn to spit little seeds to cut down the zombies as they approach. You have to tap small suns that appear to help grow new plants that you can then place on your lawn to defeat yet more zombie attacks (see Figure 12-2).

As you proceed through levels of the game, you get additional items, such as sunflowers, walnuts, and Venus flytraps, that you can use in your attempts to thwart the zombies. At some point, you're told the final wave of zombies is coming; if you survive the next minute or so, the zombies are defeated, and you get a new type of plant to use in your next defense against them.

Don't ask why. Just try it.

Figure 12-2: Oh no! Stop those zombies in their tracks!

Fruit Ninja

From: HalfBrick Studios Pty Ltd.

Price: $0.99

This game combines the concept of a ninja warrior and fresh fruit. Somehow, I believe this makes the mayhem that ensues less violent in nature. Essentially, pieces of fruit are thrown up on the screen, and you use your finger to swipe across them, cutting them in half (see Figure 12-3). The trick is that occasionally a bomb gets thrown up with the fruit and you have to be quick enough to not swipe at the bomb; otherwise, you blow it up and end the game with fruit salad everywhere.

If bombs aren't your thing, you can play the Zen mode, where you're merely slicing up fruit with no bombs involved. If you've had a hard day at the office, trust me, this one is great to work out your tensions (just imagine the fruit is, well, anybody or anything that really annoyed you today).

Figure 12-3: Who knew that slicing fruit could be so fun?

Quell Reflect

From: Fallen Tree Games

Price: $0.99

Quell is a peaceful afternoon in the park compared to some of the other games listed here. It doesn't involve bombs or zombies. Instead, you get a playing board with a small raindrop on it. You can move the raindrop up or down a row to collect the pearly objects in its path while peaceful oriental music plays in the background.

The trick is that you have to figure out how to get the raindrop to hit objects not already in its path. Sometimes, you have to shift the raindrop from one side of the board to the other, move up, then over, then down, and so on until you're in line with the object you want to hit (see Figure 12-4).

As you proceed through levels, you get new challenges that require some brain power. But the whole experience is much more relaxing and peaceful than many games you find these days.

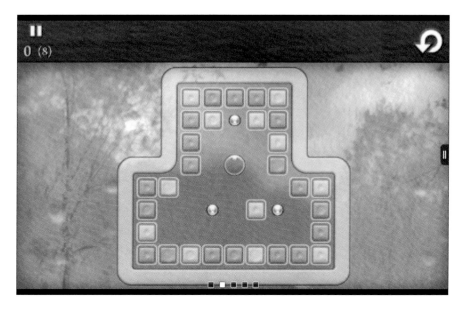

Figure 12-4: This little brain teaser will keep your mind sharp.

Airport Mania for Kindle Fire

From: Amazon Digital Services

Price: Free

Imagine you're an air traffic controller. You sit in front of your Kindle Fire screen, allowing incoming planes to land, taxi to the terminal, let passengers off, move to a holding area, and take off again. Sounds easy, right?

It is until you have five or six planes coming in and out. Then, it becomes seriously like rubbing your stomach while patting your head as a tornado approaches (see Figure 12-5). But give it a try. Nothing really crashes and nobody dies, so what can you lose?

One nice option in this game is the ability to turn the annoying music off but leave the cool sound effects on.

Figure 12-5: This game turns multitasking into an art form.

Jetpack Joyride

From: Halfbrick Studios Pty Ltd

Price: Free

If you've ever wanted to take to the skies, you must try this fun game. You ride around the virtual world using a jetpack of your choosing in the persona of Barry Streakfries, who is trying to steal cutting edge jetpacks from bad guy scientists. Tap the screen to go up into the skies or land, and use weapons in the forms of rainbows, bubbles, and lasers to win the day (see Figure 12-6).

The beauty of this game is that it really tests your reflexes as you get around obstacles in the skies and on land and avoid various physical threats.

Figure 12-6: A true classic, Jetpack Joyride takes your gaming to new heights!

Chess Free

From: Optime Software

Price: Free

If chess is your thing, you'll enjoy this electronic version. You can play the computer or play against another person using the same Kindle Fire. With the latter approach, the board swaps around after each play so that the next person can take his or her turn. There's a game timer if you're in Chess Tournament mode. You can also change the style of the pieces and board.

Tap a piece, and then the game shows you all possible moves unless you turn off Show Legal and Last Moves in the game's Options. Tap the place on the board where you want to move the piece (see Figure 12-7). If you have a change of heart, this game includes a handy Undo button.

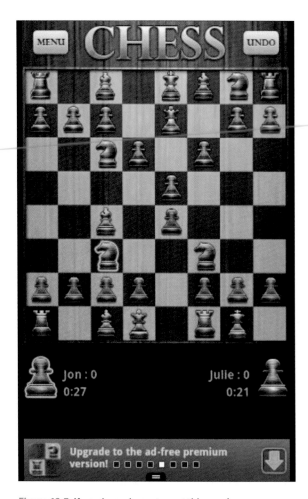

Figure 12-7: If you love chess, try out this version.

Jewels

From: MH Games/Mika Haittunen

Price: Free

If you have a thing about jewelry, or even if you don't, you might enjoy Jewels. This matching game lets you play with jewel-colored baubles to your heart's content. The idea is that you can flip two gems on this grid-like game board if doing so will allow you to line up three items of the same kind (see Figure 12-8). When you do, the lines of gems shift to provide a different arrangement.

There are a few other rules, such as getting more points for chain reactions and scoring bonus points. The game is over when there are no more possible three-of-a-kind matches left.

Figure 12-8: Simple yet colorful, Jewels promises hours of fun.

Wordsmith

From: Second Breakfast Studios

Price: $2.49

Wordsmith is kind of like the popular word game Scrabble. You build words from available tiles and take advantage of double-letter and triple-word tiles (as shown in Figure 12-9) to score extra points.

The game definitely gets you thinking about how to utilize tiles already in place to one-up yourself or your opponent. The game accommodates two to four players. Build up your vocabulary while having fun with Wordsmith.

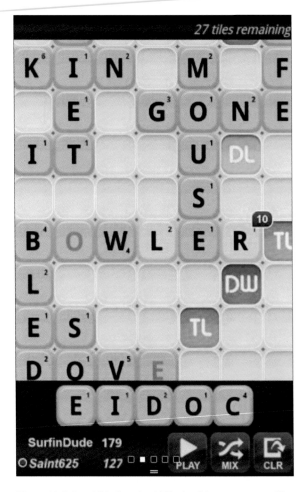

Figure 12-9: Scrabble fan alert! Wordsmith gets your spelling mojo on.

As with many games, this one comes in a free version, as well. Free versions may include advertisements and offer more limited levels of play.

Solitaire Free Pack

From: Tesseract Mobile Software

Price: Free

There aren't too many surprises to this game, but for those who are devoted to solitaire, it offers an electronic version you can play on the go on your Kindle Fire (see Figure 12-10). Rack up the points with 43 different games, including Klondike, Pyramid, and Monte Carlo.

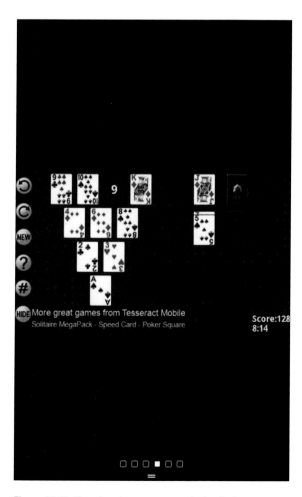

Figure 12-10: If you're alone, try a round of solitaire.

You can change the card backgrounds and track your game scores to see whether you're improving as you go. If you want to, you can take advantage of the unlimited redo feature to try and try again to win a game.

Asphalt 7: Heat

From: Gameloft

Price: $0.99

If you love to race fast cars, this game will give you that experience on your Kindle Fire HD with sharp graphics and quick moves. You can play around with more than 150 races with any of several vehicles in a wide variety of settings (see Figure 12-11). You can play locally on your Kindle Fire HD or play with up to six people online in a multiplayer environment.

Figure 12-11: Do you fancy a DeLorean, a Ferrari, or a Lamborghini? They're all available here to test drive on tracks from Paris to Hawaii.

And one for the traditional gamers

I like Random Mahjong (Paul Burkey, Free) because there are no time limits, no super bonus points to earn. You just take your time matching the nicely designed tiles layer by layer. You can control the look of the game and get hints when your brain is getting tired. This is a good way to relax between rounds of Fruit Ninja and Jetpack Joyride. Search the Games store for other old friends in the world of games; you might be surprised at what you'll find!

Beware: This game has drop-dead gorgeous graphics, but the trade off is that you'll eat up about 20MB of your device's storage.

Index

● *E* ●

Apple & Mac

iPad 2 For Dummies,
3rd Edition
978-1-118-17679-5

iPhone 4S For Dummies,
5th Edition
978-1-118-03671-6

iPod touch For Dummies,
3rd Edition
978-1-118-12960-9

Mac OS X Lion
For Dummies
978-1-118-02205-4

Blogging & Social Media

CityVille For Dummies
978-1-118-08337-6

Facebook For Dummies,
4th Edition
978-1-118-09562-1

Mom Blogging
For Dummies
978-1-118-03843-7

Twitter For Dummies,
2nd Edition
978-0-470-76879-2

WordPress For Dummies,
4th Edition
978-1-118-07342-1

Business

Cash Flow For Dummies
978-1-118-01850-7

Investing For Dummies,
6th Edition
978-0-470-90545-6

Job Searching with Social
Media For Dummies
978-0-470-93072-4

QuickBooks 2012
For Dummies
978-1-118-09120-3

Resumes For Dummies,
6th Edition
978-0-470-87361-8

Starting an Etsy Business
For Dummies
978-0-470-93067-0

Cooking & Entertaining

Cooking Basics
For Dummies, 4th Edition
978-0-470-91388-8

Wine For Dummies,
4th Edition
978-0-470-04579-4

Diet & Nutrition

Kettlebells For Dummies
978-0-470-59929-7

Nutrition For Dummies,
5th Edition
978-0-470-93231-5

Restaurant Calorie Counter
For Dummies,
2nd Edition
978-0-470-64405-8

Digital Photography

Digital SLR Cameras &
Photography For Dummies,
4th Edition
978-1-118-14489-3

Digital SLR Settings
& Shortcuts
For Dummies
978-0-470-91763-3

Photoshop Elements 10
For Dummies
978-1-118-10742-3

Gardening

Gardening Basics
For Dummies
978-0-470-03749-2

Vegetable Gardening
For Dummies,
2nd Edition
978-0-470-49870-5

Green/Sustainable

Raising Chickens
For Dummies
978-0-470-46544-8

Green Cleaning
For Dummies
978-0-470-39106-8

Health

Diabetes For Dummies,
3rd Edition
978-0-470-27086-8

Food Allergies
For Dummies
978-0-470-09584-3

Living Gluten-Free
For Dummies,
2nd Edition
978-0-470-58589-4

Hobbies

Beekeeping
For Dummies,
2nd Edition
978-0-470-43065-1

Chess For Dummies,
3rd Edition
978-1-118-01695-4

Drawing For Dummies,
2nd Edition
978-0-470-61842-4

eBay For Dummies,
7th Edition
978-1-118-09806-6

Knitting For Dummies,
2nd Edition
978-0-470-28747-7

Language &
Foreign Language

English Grammar
For Dummies,
2nd Edition
978-0-470-54664-2

French For Dummies,
2nd Edition
978-1-118-00464-7

German For Dummies,
2nd Edition
978-0-470-90101-4

Spanish Essentials
For Dummies
978-0-470-63751-7

Spanish For Dummies,
2nd Edition
978-0-470-87855-2

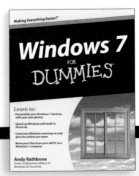
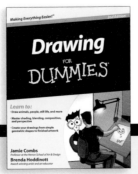

Math & Science

Algebra I For Dummies,
2nd Edition
978-0-470-55964-2

Biology For Dummies,
2nd Edition
978-0-470-59875-7

Chemistry For Dummies,
2nd Edition
978-1-1180-0730-3

Geometry For Dummies,
2nd Edition
978-0-470-08946-0

Pre-Algebra Essentials
For Dummies
978-0-470-61838-7

Microsoft Office

Excel 2010 For Dummies
978-0-470-48953-6

Office 2010 All-in-One
For Dummies
978-0-470-49748-7

Office 2011 for Mac
For Dummies
978-0-470-87869-9

Word 2010
For Dummies
978-0-470-48772-3

Music

Guitar For Dummies,
2nd Edition
978-0-7645-9904-0

Clarinet For Dummies
978-0-470-58477-4

iPod & iTunes
For Dummies,
9th Edition
978-1-118-13060-5

Pets

Cats For Dummies,
2nd Edition
978-0-7645-5275-5

Dogs All-in One
For Dummies
978-0470-52978-2

Saltwater Aquariums
For Dummies
978-0-470-06805-2

Religion & Inspiration

The Bible For Dummies
978-0-7645-5296-0

Catholicism For Dummies,
2nd Edition
978-1-118-07778-8

Spirituality For Dummies,
2nd Edition
978-0-470-19142-2

Self-Help & Relationships

Happiness For Dummies
978-0-470-28171-0

Overcoming Anxiety
For Dummies,
2nd Edition
978-0-470-57441-6

Seniors

Crosswords For Seniors
For Dummies
978-0-470-49157-7

iPad 2 For Seniors
For Dummies, 3rd Edition
978-1-118-17678-8

Laptops & Tablets
For Seniors For Dummies,
2nd Edition
978-1-118-09596-6

Smartphones & Tablets

BlackBerry For Dummies,
5th Edition
978-1-118-10035-6

Droid X2 For Dummies
978-1-118-14864-8

HTC ThunderBolt
For Dummies
978-1-118-07601-9

MOTOROLA XOOM
For Dummies
978-1-118-08835-7

Sports

Basketball For Dummies,
3rd Edition
978-1-118-07374-2

Football For Dummies,
2nd Edition
978-1-118-01261-1

Golf For Dummies,
4th Edition
978-0-470-88279-5

Test Prep

ACT For Dummies,
5th Edition
978-1-118-01259-8

ASVAB For Dummies,
3rd Edition
978-0-470-63760-9

The GRE Test For
Dummies, 7th Edition
978-0-470-00919-2

Police Officer Exam
For Dummies
978-0-470-88724-0

Series 7 Exam
For Dummies
978-0-470-09932-2

Web Development

HTML, CSS, & XHTML
For Dummies, 7th Edition
978-0-470-91659-9

Drupal For Dummies,
2nd Edition
978-1-118-08348-2

Windows 7

Windows 7
For Dummies
978-0-470-49743-2

Windows 7
For Dummies,
Book + DVD Bundle
978-0-470-52398-8

Windows 7 All-in-One
For Dummies
978-0-470-48763-1

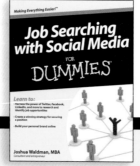

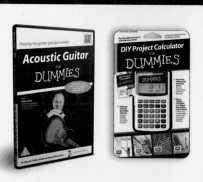